W9-BNS-772

No Greater Joy
Volume One

by

Michael & Debi Pearl

Published by
The Church At Cane Creek
1000 Pearl Road
Pleasantville, TN 37033
United States of America

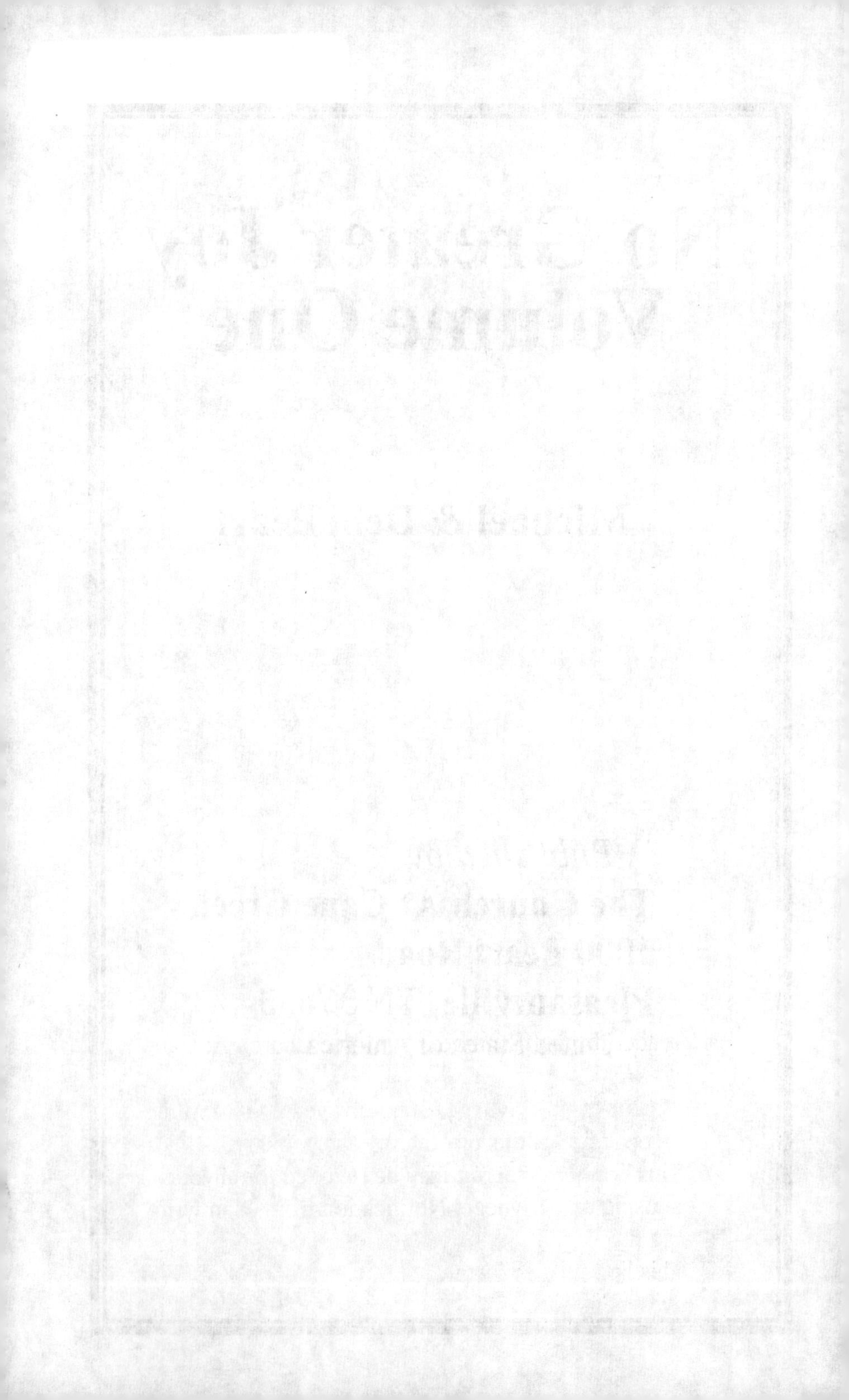

Copyright © 1997
Michael & Debi Pearl

First Printing: July 1997
Second Printing: September 1998

ISBN 1-892112-01-9

All Scripture taken from the
Authorized Version (King James) Holy Bible

This book is copyrighted by Michael & Debi Pearl. All English copies are published by The Church At Cane Creek. We grant permission for the reprint of single articles from this book on the conditions that:

1. Article must be printed in its entirety.
2. No more than one article to a publication.
3. Complete recognition be given as to the source.
4. Every reprint must include sufficient information for reader to purchase book from The Church At Cane Creek.
5. No copyright privileges are conveyed by reprinting any portion of this or other of our books.
6. This license to reprint may be revoked for anyone abusing this privilege. Notification from us in writing will negate this privilege to reprint.
7. This license is in force until the printing of a public statement otherwise.

Contents

Preface

Soon after the publication of our first book we began receiving far more mail than we could answer, so we instituted *No Greater Joy,* our monthly newsletter, to answer the most often asked questions. Subscription to the newsletter is free upon request.

Each month Deb and I answer the most pressing needs in our newsletter. Every day we receive requests for back issues, which were long since depleted. For the most part, the same questions are asked over and over again. Rather than continuing to answer the same questions, we thought it best to reprint in book form the child training articles from our first two years of newsletters.

Some of the articles have undergone minor editing. We have not attempted to group the articles in subjects. We have followed the basic order in which they were written over a two-year period. The most significant issues—those that were repeatedly asked—were dealt with several times. If we had grouped the articles into subjects, reading them consecutively would have been redundant in some cases. Rather than edit several articles on the same subject into a single shorter version, it is our thinking that the repeat may serve to reinforce the more crucial issues. By reading two or three articles each day, over several weeks the reader will experience the variety of issues in the order they developed from the questions we received from our readers.

We have included a rather thorough index that will make this an easy to use handbook.

The sale and distribution of our writings are under the auspices of our church. We do not receive any royalties. Deb and I are thankful to be privileged to serve you in this way.

A Whole Way of Life

The number of homeschoolers is rapidly increasing. Homeschooling is not just an alternative educational procedure; it is one of many expressions of a whole way of life. It is the result of loving parents putting on the brakes and saying "NO" to this stampeding system of child-trampling New Agers. A system that is inherently faulty from the start has now been shanghaied by the twisted minds of the morally ill.

Homeschooling families are determined not to be devoured and digested, becoming part of the feces of this carnivorous monster called public education.

As homeschooling parents, you have taken charge of your life with intentions of giving God his rightful place in training your children. To teach biology in an environment that denies the Author of life is like eating an egg while denying the chicken. Such a process is stupefying—degrading to the intellect. To teach history apart from God is to praise the sculpture and deny the sculptor. To learn science and mathematics apart from the omnipotent God is to throw out the computer and do your computations with a roulette wheel. To teach children to read and then outlaw the reading of the only book written by the God called *The Word* is like giving a blind man sight and then outlawing seeing.

The public school expelled God from the classroom, but when their immorality became a threat to personal satisfaction, as well as personal safety, they started talking about values. They will not get their values back any more than a man will get fruit from a tree he has severed from its roots.

We are not rebels. Quite the opposite. We are just a minority who refuse to join a rebellion against God and the truth. We are taking our children to the tree of life growing beside the fountain of knowledge to be refreshed by the Author of life. We will not stoop for anything less. We will not compromise. We will not allow state testing to dictate our curriculum. They have made their position on God and morality clear. We are making our position clear. We will not attend their party, dance to their tune or employ their fiddler. ☺

Twinkie Twerp

My wife was standing in a yard talking to the young mother of a seven-year-old boy and two girls. The girls are fairly obedient and even-tempered, but the boy is the kind that keeps my books circulating. He came from the house with a Hostess Twinkie, demanding that he have it.

His mother said, "No, there is not enough for the other children (neighbor children with whom he was playing)."

He looked shocked and offended, then anger curled his lips and hardened his brow. He began to protest and beg, frantically tearing at the wrapping. It appeared he would defiantly rip it open. The mother commenced a foot shuffling, grabbing competition for the Twinkie. For a while it was up in the air as to who would win. She finally out-grabbed him, but she didn't win—neither did the boy. He was the greater loser, a loss of character.

Since he knew that, due to her size, eventually it would be necessary to forfeit his spoils, he surrendered the Twinkie. But it was his bargaining chip. Mother was standing there holding the deformed Twinkie, looking exhausted, when he demanded, "Then, let me have a graham cracker." Seeing a way out, she paid the little extortionist his graham cracker and resumed her adult conversation. It was all in a day's stress at the old home place.

He never actually expected to overpower his mother (though he will someday). He just wanted to express his anger at being denied personal indulgence. Furthermore, from past experiences he knew how to manipulate her into compliance. After all, he did intimidate his mother into giving him a graham cracker. This mother had reinforced his ugly pattern of behavior. As we have said, "All children are trained—some positively, some negatively." She was training him to repeat this negative behavior.

Let's look at this experience a little closer. She could have handled the situation by flying into a rage and spanking him for his lousy attitude and actions. He would have screamed and kicked to make her sorry for being such an "abusive, cruel mom." She would have felt deeply defeated in spirit and, I hope, saddened by the condition of his soul. If she increased the spankings or their severity, he would be more cautious but still angry and manipulative. Is this your situation? Have you "tried everything" and concluded that you just have a "strong-willed" child? Not so. You have neglected to properly train.

Keep in mind that the Twinkie consumer's responses are a result of undisciplined desires for *"things good for food."* He is living for self-gratification and is angered when anything or anyone gets in his way. The issue is far bigger than doling out sweets. Our first concern is character development. The child may not be morally developed to the point of possessing the capacity to make value judgments, denying his flesh, but he can be *conditioned* to exercise self-restraint. If you do not condition him to get control of his passions now, when he is young, he will be out of control long before he knows that he should exercise self-discipline. Her giving-in has trained him to repeat this and other similar undesirable actions.

I will suggest a possible way to deal with the Twinkie ripper. He begins to tear at the wrapper and protest. Instead of accepting the challenge and becoming the other half of the competition, lean back and solemnly observe. Think of yourself as a judge reviewing the evidence. If he intended to open the package, he would do so. If he doesn't actually intend to forcibly open it, with no one caring to spar with him, his little performance would soon become a lonesome embarrassment. Wait until he manifests himself. When he gets it open or gives up trying, take any course of action that not only denies him immediate gratification, but denies future gratification as well. Make his actions counterproductive by responding in a way that denies him much more than what he hoped to gain (This is Rule # 1 in child training). When he gets the Twinkie out of the wrapper, calmly tell him to give it to his friends.

The shock of your cold and solemn rock hardness will probably cause him to obey. Then, tell him that he will be denied sweets for one week. Reinforce it with a spanking. Stand by your pronouncement. Let him suffer deprivation while the other family members indulge. After two or three such times, he will see the law of cause and effect in action. Apply the principle of action and reaction. When his actions are inappropriate, it is the cause of a reaction on your part that will get him the opposite of what he wanted. He will soon make adjustments, using the law to his own benefit. If you are as consistent as the "law of the Medes and the Persians," he will adjust his actions in favor of his own appetite.

What if he should continue to scream and protest when you give the Twinkie to the other children? Lead him to the place where the "magic wand" is kept and give him respect for the "Powers that be."

What if he should continue to steal sweets and make demands? Simply tell him that his actions have led you to see that his addiction must be broken, so you will not buy anything sweet for one month—and stick to it. The worst thing you could do is to make an exception or to give over after a week or two.

Moral development

You may ask, **"If he is still motivated by selfishness, how is the conditioning going to be morally beneficial?"** Though he may still be acting out of self-interest, he is caused to exercise his own will in the immediate denial of passion. This will equip him for exercising self-discipline when his moral faculties are fully developed. The rod and your manipulation of his responses can't change the child's heart. However, it can completely check the "evil" manifestations of the heart and provide a very teachable and disciplined body that is, regardless of the reason, exercising self-restraint.

The rod, when ministered with dignity and for the child's good, is an indispensable part of the training. But it cannot take the place of training. You must not continue to scream at or beat on your child in response to his repeated twinkieholism. Arrange the circumstances so that, if nothing else, his own selfishness will motivate him to acceptable behavior; and then use the rod as a part of that reinforcement and training. ☺

Why, but why?

Question: ***"My child is always asking 'Why?' What should I do?"***

When a child is told to do something that he doesn't want to do, he will often ask, "Why?" In most cases the question is not prompted by a spirit of cooperative inquiry, but by a spirit of rebellion. The question is thrown at the parent as a challenge to his or her authority, wisdom, and motive. The child's question is actually a statement of defiance. The wise parent will know that the character of the child is better served if the question is left unanswered. The child should trust the wisdom and good intentions of the parent. The issue is not a deficit of information, but a deficit of submission. The child who is perfectly compliant in spirit doesn't need explanations. Though, in some cases children may delight in knowing why because they enjoy the camaraderie of decision making. Be sensitive to discern the difference between rebellion and sincere inquiry. ☺

QUESTION: ***"My two-year-old will not stay in bed when I put him down. It seems like I am whipping him too much. No matter how many times I whip him he still gets up."***

Another parent comments:

"My little girl will not stay out of the refrigerator. Every time I turn my back, she is opening the door. I spank her, but it seems to do no good."

ANSWER: There are hundreds of issues similar to these, but the principal is the same. The child is exerting his will for the purpose of self-gratification. On one side is your displeasure and threat of discipline; on the other side is the child's consuming passion to be gratified in his "lusts." In his disobedience, he is stating that he would rather live with your displeasure and the possibility of a spanking than to be deprived of carnal satisfaction.

It is sometimes true that mothers' spankings are not at all

painful. If your spankings are too light to gain his respect, an increase in the intensity might be more persuasive. If the child deemed the pain to be worse than the gratification, he would grudgingly stop. However, our goal is much deeper than just keeping the door shut on the refrigerator. We want to train our children to control their passions. We can "outgun" them, but the power play is limited by the child's inability to remember and make associations. That is, when the child is possessed of the strength of passion (getting out of bed, opening the refrigerator, etc.), he cannot reason and remember the severe consequences. He is acting on immediate impulse—just like an undisciplined adult dominated by his lust. Think of an alcoholic, a drug addict, or a glutinous person. I have observed diabetics go to a church dinner and gorge themselves on sweets, oblivious to their spouses standing behind them warning of the consequences. The diabetic is able to rationalize because there have been those rare occasions when he has indulged without dire consequences. If he can get away with the sweets one time out of ten, then he will eat hoping that this will be the rare exception. It is not smart, but it is human. I say *human* derogatorily.

Where you have been inconsistent with your child—that is you occasionally allow him to triumph in the pursuit of his rebellion—he will focus his lust on that one time when it paid off, and will barge ahead, hoping that this will be another permissive exception. If, once every two weeks, his getting out of bed is rewarded by being allowed to join the adults in that cozy time of late evening, he will keep facing the switch until he is again rewarded or until his memory of the fruitfulness of such an act grows dull. When it is NEVER A PLEASURABLE EXPERIENCE to get out of bed, his own self-love will cause him to stay in bed.

By your consistency, you will eventually condition the child to always submit to authority. If there is even one area where a child is consistently rebellious, you have a child totally self-willed at heart. If he is allowed to choose the areas of obedience, he is, in fact, never submitted to any authority but his own.

Rather than harder spankings, I would suggest that you determine to be absolutely consistent. Make sure that he is sleepy, and then put him to bed with a Bible story, a little hugging, and a prayer. Be sure he knows he is to stay in bed. Then do for him as you would want done for you—keep the house quiet so he can sleep. Meanwhile, be very attentive. If he gets up, when his feet hit the floor, spring into the room with your little switch and pop him on the bare leg one or two times. No anger on your part—no raised voices. Just make it more pleasant to stay in bed. Never allow him to get his way. One week of consistency on your part will convince him that this business is under new management.

Be creative. The child who is opening the refrigerator obviously wants something to eat. If you never, never, I SAY NEVER allow it to be a rewarding experience, he will stop. If he gets less to eat rather than more, he will deem it beneficial to his appetite to ignore the refrigerator. For example, if the child is getting into the cheese, tell him that he can't have cheese even at meal times. And then stand by your word. When the other children eat cheese, he can eat dry bread for a week. He is not stupid. His appetite will keep the door closed. You must be absolutely consistent if he is to be consistent. There is no place for reprieve in this training. Don't try to whip your inconsistencies out of your children. Train them right and they will always obey. ☺

Emotional Manipulators

Just this week a family was visiting us in the herb garden while their children played in the yard. The delicate little four-year-old girl was pouty and moody. For a while she just watched the other children having fun but didn't participate. She was the smallest and often couldn't keep up. Eventually she made an attempt to chase after the others. So doing, she fell on the thick carpet of grass and immediately began to scream as if the goat was eating her favorite hat. She followed up the pitiful scream with a desperate run to her mother. "Poor child." The mother, drawn by the "tragedy," did what all mothers are expected to do: she sympathetically rushed to her wounded child. The four-year-old psychologist was well aware that, with others looking on, her mother's reputation was at stake.

Though it was not outwardly visible, I knew the mother was irritated at her child. She didn't actually feel sympathetic. She was probably thinking something like: "What's wrong with the little brat now? She's such a crybaby. I know she is not really hurt. Why does she pretend to be?" And then the guilt feelings hit the mother and she lies to herself: "Oh well, she is just a little thing, and even though there is no scratch or bruise, and the ground is not hard, maybe she is hurt."

The mother intuitively knows that what she is hearing is not a cry of pain, but of protest. She can't sort out her thoughts and feelings, so she follows social custom and pretends to be concerned. The mother's aggravated pretense conceals undefined feelings, putting steam in a boiler that will later, in private, boil over into anger and irritability toward her child. In this situation the mother doesn't like her child. This causes her to feel inadequate because she knows that her attitude renders her unfit to properly mother her own child. In truth, the thing that irritates and even disgusts this mother is actually a developing character flaw in her child.

By her mother's responses, this little girl has been trained to be an emotional manipulator. When she can't get her way, she pretends to be hurt—or takes a small hurt and makes it into a big one. Mother rushes to her child, rewarding every cry with special attention and rewarding every complaint of abuse with a demand that she be allowed to play. Other children don't like a "crybaby" who forces limitations on their play.

Boys can be crybabies as well. When he begins to scream his defiance or hurt, just ignore him. Don't be moved by it. Don't pick him up. Tell him, "There is no reason to cry, so go away and play." If he demands attention to a supposed wound, then reach in your purse, pull out a terrible tasting herbal potion and give him a spoon full. After he gets through gagging on the vitamin and mineral supplement, tell him that he is now completely healed and invite him to come back for another dose if he again gets hurt. If you don't have a horrible tasting herbal remedy, use something that is very unpleasant, yet good for the child—like apple cider vinegar with garlic. Don't laugh while he is looking. Remember, you are doctoring a serious attitude problem. Three doses are guaranteed to forever cure emotional manipulators and also prevent the development of future hypochondriacs. If crying and running to mom does not advance his agenda over others, he will learn to make his own way and accept the normal unfairness and hardships of life. Everyone will like him better, including his own brothers and sisters. Furthermore, he will be happier. The only ones who will suffer from being firm and aloof toward crybabies are the mothers, and sometimes fathers, who will not have their own needs meet in responding to the "poor" child. ☺

Potty Training Answered

In our book, To Train Up A Child, the chapter that has produced the most inquires is the one on potty training infants. The letters have ranged from those who challenge our integrity for making such a bragging claim to those who thank us for the success they have seen in potty training their own infants. We often laughingly joke about the wisdom of adding it to the book. But for those of you who have been successful, it's worth it. To the rest of you struggling, frustrated moms, forgive us; it was just an idea to make life easier, not harder. Potty training infants is certainly not character building. This article is in answer to all of you who have written, asking for more detail.

While on mission trips in Central America, I noticed that the tribal women did not put diapers on their babies. I found this interesting and started asking questions. Occasionally, mothers would slide their babies out of their back slings and sit them on the tops of their feet. The babies, being put in that position, then relieved themselves on the ground. I had read about this being done in the forties by Jewish mothers working to build the nation of Israel. Then, when I saw it being done in C.A., it provoked me to try it with my own babies. Of course, I had to modify the method somewhat.

When my next child was born, I put a cloth diaper on her and laid her on my tummy. In this position, during those first few days of recovery, when I felt the diaper getting warm, I gave the action a name. My newborn came to associate the word I spoke with the release of her muscles. For the first few months, I put her on the seat in front of me so she would feel secure and relaxed. By waiting until I judged her bladder to be full, when I spoke the appropriate word she just released her muscles and repeated the action she had come to associate with the word.

In the early stage, I dribbled cold water down her tummy to stimulate her to "peepee." All the external stimuli worked together to provoke a response—the cold seat against her warm legs, the position of her body, the words I spoke, the dribbled water, and her full bladder. My two older children helped, and sometimes even Daddy. It was a ritual about ever two or three hours. When we failed to perceive her need and discovered a bowel movement or peepee in progress, we still rushed her to the pot, saying the appropriate word to reinforce the association. She caught on quickly, and by the time she was three months old she would fuss when she needed to go. Until she was about one year old, any time we were out in public for any length of time, I put a diaper on her just in case of an accident.

I have often wondered if I would have had the same success if I had tried this on my first child. She had many bowel movements each day—often while nursing. Since I only trained the two younger girls, I don't know how it would work with boys. In our child training seminars, we have met other mothers who boast of success with their babies. We have the moms stand and take a bow while we all applaud. Having older children to assist you is a great advantage.

It was never, NEVER a discipline matter. If you wait until the child is three or four months old to attempt training, it may be more difficult because you are working against a learned habit.

Well, go have another baby and give it a try. Let us know if you have success. We have heard of enough failures. On the other hand, what's a little diaper rash and a pail full of stinky diapers? After all, it's an American tradition. What other ways do you have to spend your time? ☹

Don't Give Up

Homeschooling parent, do you sometimes (maybe all the time) feel that you are in over your head? You are not alone. Anyone who takes responsibility will feel the weight of responsibility. The home-schooling mom and dad are psychologically handicapped before they start. They are given cause to feel inadequate.

Public education is operated by tradesmen. In any trade, the tradesmen must create the illusion that they alone have the skills or knowledge to meet your need. Only in the last century has the education of children been turned over to the professionals. As a result, the parent's natural teaching skills are dormant.

I am reminded of the child reared by a deranged spinster who didn't want her "baby" to grow up. She lived to be needed. She never let him feed himself. At six years old, he had never placed food in his own mouth. When she suddenly died and left him locked in a remote old house, he nearly starved to death before someone found him. There was plenty of food, but he did not feel adequate to feed himself. The professionals have made themselves indispensable by their spoon feeding the sacred knowledge. They would have us believe that only university graduates can provide proper educational nourishment. Experience proves that children develop best at their own mother's breast.

From the teachers themselves, we hear about the failure of the corporate classroom. If you listen to the professionals when they are called upon to explain their failure, you will hear them blame overcrowded classrooms. Do any of you have overcrowded classrooms? They tell us they can't spend enough time one-on-one. Do you have twenty-five students to prevent you from spending time with one who needs extra attention? They will excuse their lack of control in the classroom by pointing to the laws that prevent them from exercising discipline. For the present, we homeschool parents are still free to discipline.

I have heard the public school spokesmen explain their failures by complaining that there is not enough parental involvement. We homeschoolers don't have any problem there. They also tell us that a breakdown in the family structure is to blame. Homeschool, by its very nature, is a strong family structure. Also, we are told that many children have special needs, requiring special care. Homeschool moms and dads are the most astute specialists in the world, prompted by the fact that they are working with someone who is very special to them.

You may ask, "If I have all these advantages, why do I feel so inadequate?" Has it ever occurred to you that the beginning public school teachers also feel inadequate? Have you ever felt inadequate in other areas where you have launched out into something new? The more something matters to us the more we demand of ourselves and the greater our self-criticism. When you consider the criticism of relatives, suspicious neighbors, and the State threat, it's a wonder any of us persist.

Remember, your feelings are just your feelings. They are not a true reflection of how well you are actually doing. You can't control involuntary feelings, but you can continue, knowing that nearly every successful homeschool parent has felt the same as you.

Don't push too hard or too soon. That which takes months to teach a six-year-old can be taught to an eight-year-old in a few days. Some children mature in cognitive skills several years ahead of their peers. Others mature several years behind the average. The ones who mature earlier are not necessarily brighter than the late bloomers. It's a mistake to allow standards set by early achievers to be imposed upon you and your children.

Don't permit pride to cause anxiety about your child's public performance. Your knowledge that the grandparents are going to put your seven or eight-year-old up on their laps and open a book that he can't read can cause you to be impatient. Resist being controlled by the opinions of others. It is one thing to be concerned that your child is not developing as he should. It is quite another to be concerned for what others think about your child's development. The former can motivate you. The latter will depress you and cause you to exert undue and unnatural pressure on your children—thus retarding their learning. ☺

Schooling, What Age?

Children are put in classrooms where they are continually bombarded with information and tested as to their progress. They never learn all the material, but the same information, becoming slightly more complex each year, is continually thrown at them. It takes twelve long, hard years to drum curriculum into them which, later in their development, they could learn in two years. The system has been arranged so that as soon as a child's mental development will allow comprehension of even a small amount of the material, he is made responsible for it. It reminds me of an Alaskan farmer going out to dig fence postholes in frozen ground. Being in a hurry, each day, as the thawing permits, he chops away at the frozen ground, digging a little deeper. After a long Spring, tired muscles, and much frustration, he finally gets the holes dug. On the same day, his next door neighbor, having waited until the ground was ready, dug all his post holes in one day—the same day the first farmer finished.

Because some children are ready to begin learning to read between the ages of four and six, this has been accepted as the time to start all children. The early maturing children have been allowed to set the pace for the average children. The later maturing children, one or two years behind the others, though just as bright, are always under a pile trying to keep up. In that competitive environment, they develop a sense of inadequacy. If they are not crushed by a belief in their failure, the later maturing children may prove to be the brightest when they are grown. The haste of the professional educator is like moving into a house before it is finished. If you wait until the children's mental faculties are amply developed, in a nurturing environment they will have a natural craving to learn. At the right time, if the child's soul has not been scarred by premature stress, teaching is easy.

For the sake of understanding, observe with me an imaginary experiment with two children of equal mental comprehension. Both are destined to mature at the same time. The one in a traditional classroom will be continually pushed to his limit. Before he is ready, he will be made responsible for certain information. He will comprehend some of it right away, but much of it will just trouble him until he matures to the point of comprehension. For the teacher it is sometimes like piling dry sand. It is a seemingly endless process of hammering it in—drill and test, drill and test. As the student develops new mental rooms, the teacher waits outside to fill them with information. He is not ready for most of what is thrown at him, but they just keep slinging it in his direction until it sticks. The poor child is a professional student at six years old. He is filled with responsibilities and worries. Being away at school, he has no mother to comfort him. If he is at home, and it is his mother who is placing these burdens on him, then his comforter has become his tormentor.

The other child in our experiment is at home at his mother's feet feeling secure and protected. He is mentally developing at the same pace, but his information rooms are not being bombarded and tested before they are complete. If asked academic questions, he may appear to be two or three years behind the other child in our experiment. At seven or eight this child will begin learning the school

material that our other child was learning at six. The difference is that where it took five hours a day to teach the six-year-old, it takes only one hour a day to teach the eight-year-old the same material. And most significant, our eight-year-old homeschooler is loving every minute of it. He is not being burnt-out by pressure and competition. He is not struggling to learn. His hunger is just being fed. The homeschool parent who is willing to wait for the mental and emotional development to occur will experience far less frustration and anxiety, and the child will have fun learning. I have observed that by the time homeschooled children are fourteen or fifteen they have far surpassed their traditionally schooled counterparts—and that with one-tenth the effort. ☺

Of Utmost Concern

I think many of you feel as I do. My most important personal concern is my children. Even before I was married, my occupation, financial security, ministry, personal fulfillment, all took third place to concerns for my future children. *"What does it profit a man if he gain the whole world and lose his own soul?"* In addition, what does it profit a man if he gains the whole world and loses the soul of his children?

What can be called success if your children turn out to be part of the world's problem rather than its cure? What satisfaction can there be in the comforts of material success if your children grow up needing counsel rather than being sought after to give counsel? If your children lie awake at night suffering from guilt and anxiety, being gnawed on by the demons of intemperance and self-indulgence, how can you enjoy your food or your pillow?

The success of a tree or a man is measured by the fruit that is borne. The fruit of a man or woman is their children; everything else is falling leaves.

If the sun rises and sets and I cast no bigger shadow, what of it, if my children are growing in God's family? Let me die poor; let me die early; let me be ravaged by disease; but let my children rise up and call me blessed. Let me not measure my giving by the dollars I spend on them or the educational opportunities that my station in life affords them, but rather, by the hours we spend in fellowship.

May they graduate from my tutorship to become disciples of the Man from Nazareth. May they know good and evil from the pinnacle of obedience rather than from the pit of despair. May they have the wisdom to choose the precious and the courage to reject the trite and the vain. May they always labor for the meat that endures.

May they be lovers of God, coworkers with the Holy Spirit, and a friend to the Lord Jesus. And when their trail ends, may it end at the throne of God laying crowns at the Savior's feet. ☺

The Emotional Squeeze

I just received a call from a young mother who tries very hard to properly rear her children. They are very obedient and pleasant. However, she has one concern. Her little three-year-old girl seems to be fearful and anxious when disciplined. She seems to withdraw into an "I'm being hurt mood." There is no rebellion. There is instant compliance. When spanked, she stands rigid and stoically accepts her "just due." Afterwards, however, she looks anxious and fearful.

I asked the mother if she is expressing hostility or anger toward her daughter. She answered as I expected (knowing the family well), "No, I am not angry or impatient. I always take a long time and explain how she has done wrong and why I am spanking her." So I asked the mother, "Does she begin to be withdrawn and hurt before the spanking?" "Yes, as soon as I begin to talk to her, she acts like she is going into some kind of a trance or something. She just acts like it is hurting her so much to be rebuked. If I tell her to stop crying, she does. If I tell her to smile, she does, but I don't feel like I am getting through to her soul."

Just to make sure of what I already believed, I asked and she assured me that she was spending time building her child up as a worthy and valuable member of the family.

So, as we evaluate this mother's concern, note that she is not concerned that her child obey, or even that she have a good attitude; this she does. She is concerned for what is going on behind those cold, misted eyes, which ultimately is our deepest concern. Let a child get rowdy, fail to do his chores, tear something up, steal a cookie, hit his sister over the head with her favorite teddy bear, or sneak off to play with an undesirable neighbor; but make sure that the lights burning behind the windows of that little soul are bright and honest.

In such a situation as this, my first thought is to search out any emotional or physical abuse. That trance-like, non-resistant submission is symptomatic of a child scared to death. That not being a possibility here, I was puzzled until she told me that the child began to withdraw as soon as the lecture began. I have seen this situation many times before. It occurs as a result of an intense, oversensitive mother or father—usually mother. A mother who is consumed with her own deep feelings will project that same emotional seriousness into every personal confrontation. Have you met people to whom you wanted to say, "Lighten up, relax; It's not that serious yet?"

Don't overwork your child's emotions with excessive indulgence in: "Why did you do that? You hurt Mother. You make me feel so badly. What you did is wrong, and God wants us to love our neighbor, etc." Children, especially young children, are not equipped to deal with deep issues of motive and duty. The degree to which they are morally awakened should be addressed; but to expose them to the adult burden of motive and responsibility can cause them to carry too much of a burden. Children can become depressed and withdrawn when they know they are about to go through another emotionally heavy grilling, which to them only spells rejection. If they had the courage to speak, they would plead, "Whip me double time, but stop whining and looking at me with that forlorn pitiful expression." Children can take the spankings and bounce back before you find a place to lay the switch. But your emotions can bury them under a pile. Save the deep hurt and serious lectures for those rare times when the offense is worthy of Hell. Don't take them to the judgment seat of Christ every time they act like kids.

This mother confessed that when she wanted the children to do something, she would *ask* them to do it rather than *tell* them. They were left with the responsibility of deciding whether or not they should act. In some cases, when the mother really was giving them a choice, they found that they could say "No" and the mother let it slide. But at other times the mother expected the children to obey her "suggestions." When the children fail to agree to do what is "asked," the mother just sighs deeply and assumes a look of being personally hurt. The children are then expected to evaluate their mother's pain and alter their course accordingly. Of course, the children will eventually be emotionally manipulated into following the mother's feelings. This is beginning to get sick.

Hey! Where is the old fashioned "Mama says pick up your clothes in the next thirty seconds"? No emotion, no alternative, no mercy. "In this household there is one 'law of the Medes and the Persians, which changeth not' and I am it. You now have three seconds and counting." The mother is not angry. She is not hurried. She is smiling. The kid muses, "I think she is hoping I don't make it in time. I believe she is going to enjoy spanking me. Get out of my way sister, I am coming down the hall with a load of dirty clothes at about sixty miles an hour." As the little tot dives into the clothes hamper with his pile of laundry, the mother makes a little buzzer sound with her mouth, laughs and lays her switch down, saying, "You made it this time. Oh well, maybe next," and turns to another chore. The kid backs out of the clothes hamper, laughs and feels like he just won at some sort of competition. He feels secure because his mother is secure. He may get half a dozen little spankings a day, but he never has to deal with weighty emotional matters that are meant only for adults. ☺

Marketplace Success

Few parents have the bold confidence to care more for their children's happiness than for their marketplace success. Marketplace success with all its inherent trappings seems to be the antitheses of happiness. No one ever wrote poetry about it. No one ever credited success with saving a marriage or encouraging the children. We have never heard of one on his death bed wishing he had spent more time in business. Success in the market place is its own end, valued for the experience itself. It is hedonistic, a trip that is satisfying to the ego. It is a pitiful measure of a man, but one by which many secure their identity. Those who sacrifice to pass on wealth to their children usually sacrifice their children. Those who sacrifice their children's youth to professional education, with the goal of marketplace success, sacrifice their children on an altar of vanity. ☹

Family Productions

I recently met a little three-year-old girl who is the product of life with her parents. The family stayed in our home for three days, and I got to know them very well. In two days of watching eyebrows and shoulder postures you can learn much about a family. Let me relate the circumstances of this little girl's three years in the school of character development.

Since she was born, her family of eight has lived four or five different places. One recent apartment was only two rooms. They told about huddling in one room for warmth because they were without electricity. The plumbing on the third floor was so bad that their water often didn't work. They had to carry it to the rundown building. The neighborhood in which they lived suffered 80% unemployment. Crime was rampant. Nearly all of the family's friends were atheists or infidels of one sort or another. The mother is busy homeschooling the older children and cannot spend excessive time on this little one. She is often shoved aside to make room for chores.

For a year her older brother was so sick that when he finally got to a doctor, the doctor expressed amazement that he was still alive. With proper treatment, the boy eventually recovered. At the present and for the last several months they have been homeless. The wife is eight months pregnant with her seventh child, and they live out of a van, going from place to place. Some of you have complained about your circumstances. You have the idea that if the environment could just be modified, things would be better. I doubt that any of my readers have had it as rough as this family.

You may ask, "Why does the family live like that; why doesn't the father provide something better?" They live that way out of love for others and obedience to their employer. The six children, from the three-year-old to the seventeen-year-old boy, are all bright, energetic, thankful and creative. They speak several languages and are all committed to getting the gospel to those who have never heard. They are missionaries to Albania.

When they went there in 1992, the country was suffering from the aftershocks of communism. The people had rioted and destroyed their own country. Food was scarce and utilities were usually inoperative. The country had boasted of being the only entirely atheistic state. No religious people of any kind could be found. They had either been killed or imprisoned. It was into this environment that God called this family to labor for the harvest. They have now returned to the States to rest and share their work with others before going back to Albania.

Now, back to the little three-year-old. Her name is Janell Rogers and she has become my new sweetheart. I first met her sitting at a long table in a missionary conference. After talking with my wife, she tapped me on the arm and asked, "Do you really have a live horse at home?" I said, "Yea, we have two of them." She looked distressed, "Where do you keep them?" "Oh they are just hanging around the back door." "Are you sure you have two live, really live horses hanging at your house," she distressingly pleaded. Her concern increased as she learned that there were live chickens, cows, cats, dogs, and other various live creatures. By now I was perplexed, for I knew that Albania was full of draft animals. Deliveries, even in the large cities, are often made on donkey back.

Finally, with her spoon dripping food, suspended in front of her bobbing head, she turned to my wife and impatiently demanded, "Do you know what *alive* means?" We eventually solved the dilemma. Before going to Albania they had been missionaries in Paraguay for eleven years. She had been reared in a multilingual home where they were active learning new languages. She somehow thought that *live* meant *dead*. She thought that our yard was full of poor dead animals. You could tell that this little world traveler was exercising extra patience on these dumb Americans.

I usually write about problem parents who produce problem children. In this case, I spent three days with a family that was able to teach us a few things. I love to make suggestions to parents about rearing their children, but in three days I couldn't find anything that needed correcting.

They had not read our book. The children were the product of two people who loved each other and of a family with habits of giving and serving. This was not a self-centered family. They were not "saving their lives," they were laying down their lives and their family for others. As a result of the Divine law of sowing and reaping, by *giving* they were *saving* their family. I would rather live in a crowded, one bedroom apartment in a foreign and sometimes hostile culture with six singing children than secure in America in a spacious home with each child in their own self-indulgent, pouty mood.

I misled you by describing their physical circumstances. You were thinking, "What a poor, disadvantaged child." I want you to see that it is not what is without, but what is within that makes good kids. By your letters I can see that many of you need to stop praying for circumstances to improve, and instead, make a family commitment to serve others. If you are too tied down trying to survive to have time to serve others, you need to do the serving more than others need your service. When we spend more time and energy giving, our own needs diminish in proportion to our concern for the needs of others. Our worry fades to the degree that we are concerned for others. Our greatest trials are born in a self-centered heart.

Giving, caring parents create giving, caring children. Frustrated, anxious and fearful parents reproduce themselves. Bitter mothers who teach their daughters to be sweet and kind still produce bitter daughters. More is caught than taught. Critical, impatient fathers train up disrespectful bullies, unworthy of a mother's love.

The first step in child training is to decide what you want your child to become and then become that very person yourself. The second principle of child training is don't complain or be surprised when they turn out to be just like you. ☺

Are you a single mother?

"The LORD preserveth the strangers; he relieveth the fatherless and widow (Psalm 146:9)."

Noah and Elijah on the Mount

Some good friends of mine dropped off their twenty four month old son to stay with us for a week while they worked in a youth camp. You can imagine the kind of screaming we expected from this situation. But, when the father introduced us, little Elijah's face became a glow of wonder as he studied my long, gray, nearly white beard. Because of the likeness to a picture in a Bible story-book his father had been reading to him, he thought I was Noah. I could see right away that he was gratified to finally meet the man who talked with God and made a big boat to save all the animals. I looked into two believing, crystal blue eyes set in a brilliant white cotton ball of blond hair and just knew I was Noah.

Well, I found out how Paul and Barnabas felt when the people of Lystra were about to do sacrifice to them. Yes sir, for a week, I was Noah the Great. When I got out of his sight, he would call for Noah. When he got up in the morning, he would go through the house calling my new name. When I carried him down to the pond to show him the fish, he uttered one of his rare words, "Boat?" And not a boat in sight. I think he thought the fish and water were left-overs from the flood; he had already observed animals in the yard.

Later that day, he cried when he didn't get to sit by me at the dinner table. Like a grandfather, spoiling the kids rotten, I rear-ranged the whole table for him (well, maybe for me).

I didn't get much cooperation from the rest of the family. On several occasions, I thought I was going to have to ring my daugh-ters' necks for calling me *Dad*. The kid probably knew that Noah only had sons.

It was great! I got to be a Daddy Noah for a week. It has been a while. What an opportunity you fathers still have to mold a little fellow into a great man of God. Children are not born with hang-ups, hostility, bitterness, or resentment. Such trappings are gleaned from the family in which they are cultured. Neither are they born hard working, kind, considerate, and godly gentlemen. Those char-acter traits are the result of sixteen or eighteen years of conscien-tious nurturing in the Spirit of God by a pair of loving examples. ☺

Rule of Law

Question: ***"Should a mature ten-year-old be allowed to switch a two-year-old if the mother is unavailable—for example, during a temper tantrum?"***

If children are not old enough or mature enough to spank their younger brothers and sisters, they are not qualified to be the temporary guardians. A child should never be left in the care of one who is not trusted to assume authority to spank when needed. If you can't trust them to execute discipline then you can't trust them to be the primary caretakers of your children. If a child is ever left in the presence of one who does not have full authority, you are granting the child a dispensation of unrestrained rebellion. When one child says to another, "You can't tell me what to do, you are not my mother," you can be sure the mother can't tell the child what to do either.

True submission comes from the heart and is not restricted to one or two feared authority figures. Every mature person knows there is an inherent rule of law to which we are all obligated. Children grow into this awareness, holding each other responsible to do what they know they ought. This understanding of right and wrong was placed in us at creation (Gen. 3:22) and is enforced by what we see in nature (Rom. 1:19-20) as well as by direct moral revelation from Jesus Christ (John 1:9). The children reared in Christian families have the added light of Scripture and godly example. This does not make them more righteous, just more responsible.

Just as adults, children are often tempted to ignore the dictates of conscience and to pursue a course of self-gratification, which is rebellion. As their understanding of moral obligation emerges, they must be taught and disciplined to follow this law of love and good will. If they are caused to view their obligation as extending no further than their parents, then they are given the false impression that their parents are the highest law. If the child is led to believe that the law emanates from the will of the parents alone, then law is viewed as arbitrary and temporary, which means the law can be broken when the parent is unaware. Children should be taught that there are no exceptions to their obligations; they are never out from under the law of love, decency, goodness, kindness, respect, etc. No matter who reminds them of their duty, whether it is a younger child or a stranger, they should recognize the authority of a law higher than all earthly authority, and bow in submission. To rebel against another who is attempting to enforce that law is to rebel against God who placed this law in all men.

Ten-year-olds ought to be mature enough to discipline a smaller child. If they are not, one of the things that will help them mature is to give them real responsibility over the small children. If you want to breed hostility and cause divisions in the family, just put a ten-year-old in charge of a four-year-old and forbid the ten-year-old from disciplining the younger child. He or she will despise the rebellious child and resent being put in that position. It is totally irresponsible to all parties involved to place a child under one whose hands are tied. In our house, there was no difference between the parents and the older children in enforcing the rule of law over the younger children. I supported the commands of my twelve-year-old over my four-year-old just as I did the commands of my wife. Of course, in the rare event that there was a difference, the parents' position unquestionably prevails over the older siblings.

Even parents should be humble enough to be open to their children's entreaty if they should violate this understood moral code of conduct. ☺

Screaming

Question: "My three-year-old daughter often screams when she is aggravated by the other children or when she doesn't get her way. Is this normal? Will she grow out of it?"

It is average, but not normal. As she develops a social awareness she will grow out of the screaming, but it will be replaced by more subtle tantrums to get her way.

It is an easy habit to break. When she starts screaming, before you find out who is at fault, without saying a word, go straight to the switch. Spank her where she stands, and then inquire concerning the problem. Explain to her that the screaming will never again be allowed. When she is convinced that screaming will never get the other children in trouble, never gain her any sympathy—only a spanking—she will cease using screaming to gain her way. You might just ignore any offense from the others when she screams; let it always be her fault.

Consistency on your part will break that habit in just a few days. Never threaten, and never show mercy. One squeak of a scream gets a switching. If you are consistent, four to eight episodes should bring it to an end. If you are 95% consistent and find it more convenient to only warn her occasionally, or if she finds that, regardless of the spanking, she is occasionally able to get her way by screaming, then it should only take about eighteen years to break the habit. Actually, it won't be broken, but when she is married you won't have to listen to her scream any more. It will be her husband's problem then. But, by then, you will have realized the mistake of being only 95% consistent, and you can practice on your grandchildren. No doubt, they will be screamers just like their mother. ☹

Sibling Aggression

Question: "How do you handle sibling aggression, fighting over toys, etc.? How do they learn to handle situations and not run to Mama? How does Mama learn not to intervene?"

You must first recognize the right of private property. If two families shared the same yard, they would soon fuss over how it is to be used. If six families had joint ownership over one car, how long would they go before fighting? Don't expect your children to show a level of maturity and sacrifice that few adults ever display.

Where it becomes a problem, permit no joint ownership. Do

not force a child to give over his rights. The owner has prior rights no matter who had it first. That settles 95% of the conflicts before they arise. If there must be joint ownership, then it will have to be handled on a lease basis. It belongs to Jack in the morning and to Jill in the afternoon—or some other easily manageable plan. We want them to learn to give up their rights, but they can't give up rights they don't possess. Giving up is voluntary, which means they can't be pressured into compliance and still reap positive character development. If neither of them has a right to possess it, neither can give up rights.

To give a child first-come first-served right to everything in the house is to create a false worldview. It makes whiners and breeds selfishness and aggression. It does more for character building to voluntarily recognize someone else's right and give up the coveted object than it does to get to it first and selfishly possess it for no other reason than a timely possession.

"How do we handle aggression, fighting over toys?" If it is a fussing, pulling match, establish ownership. If there is no owner, lease it out or throw it away. However, if a child resorts to actual violence, hitting, biting, kicking, shoving, etc., then the violence should be dealt with by rebuke, exhortation, and a thorough spanking. Children must be taught that violence is never an acceptable alternative in personal conflicts. The rod with rebuke is a most effective teacher. ☺

The Volleyball Bawler

As the father left the volleyball court, headed for his house, his little four-year-old daughter began to scream. I was standing close enough to hear every word she uttered—about one hundred yards away. You must be gifted to interpret the *Screamer* language. If you are academically slow, this gift may not come until about the third child. It is a primitive language, rooted in primordial, selfish animal instinct. Her scream was an angry protest, demanding to be allowed to go with her father to the house. With my gift of interpretation, I understood her to be saying, "Who do you think you are running off and leaving me standing here? If you think I can be ignored without penalty, you have another thing coming. You will hold me in high esteem, or I will make you wish you had." I am sure he was quite willing to take her along. It had just not occurred to him that she might want to go. She had probably tried to get his attention and failed, due to the noise of the game. So, she resorted to what I know to be her old standby. The look on her face and the clenching of her fists projected an air of defiance and anger. I am sure that if she had been big enough, she would have run up and bopped her daddy on the side of his head to teach him a lesson about her importance.

As she gets older and becomes more socially conscious, she will learn to control her outbursts. But the habit of emotionally manipulating those around her will continue. As an adult, she will whine and complain when things don't go her way. She will have very sensitive feelings. Those closest to her will have to tread lightly, allowing her to have her way, or she will be so hurt and pitiful that they will be sorry for not showing more concern for her needs. She will use her hurt feelings as a lever to control those around her.

Back to our story. When the father turned around, the little girl immediately stopped screaming . He walked over, took her hand, and led her up the lane about one hundred yards where he stopped to give her a switching. He then permitted her to go to the house with him.

You may think, “Well, he did right; he punished her for her bad attitude.” I will have you know that she is often punished for her screaming, but she goes right on screaming. She throws so many fits that if they were all pilled into a big heap it would make a volcano.

This event well illustrates the difference between punishment and training. This child was punished for screaming and at the same time trained to scream. If you had a dog that jumped on you, demanding something to eat, and you responded by giving him the food and then whipping him for jumping, you would be punishing the dog for jumping and at the same time rewarding him for jumping.

This little girl screamed because she wanted to go to the house with her daddy. It worked. He turned around, came back, took her hand, and led her to the house where she got the special attention she wanted. That victorious moment of seeing the effectiveness of her scream confirmed and ingrained the habit of screaming. She initiated an act designed to get results. The father responded as was her intention, and the girl was trained to repeat the screaming. The later punishment did not undo the programming that had already occurred. The little four-year-old did not recall the memory of screaming and associate it with the spanking. She was punished, but, to her, punishment is just routine. She expects to be spanked periodically. It is just another opportunity to scream and make her father feel guilty.

A child does not have the adult’s ability to intellectually process information and recall it at critical moments. When this little girl is again in a position to demand her own way, the first response that comes to her mind will be to scream, because it has always worked to her advantage in the past.

How can we train her not to scream? Apply Rule #1. It always works on every child, every time. The principle is the same. She screams because it works. If it didn't work, she wouldn't scream. If the parents and other caretakers would see to it that screaming is always counterproductive, she will cease screaming forever. When we employ the rod on these young ones, we do so as part of the training, not punishment. If you are a foster parent for the government child-care system, therefore not allowed to spank, you can still train them not to scream, though with more difficulty.

Here's how you might handle this situation. As the screaming commences, walk back to the child. Stand with your hands on your hips and stare (body language). After you have raked her with disapproval, ask, "Why are you screaming, did you get snake bit?" She says, "No, I didn't want you to leave me." You respond, "Oh, I see, you screamed thinking that I would take you with me. Well, I would be delighted for you to go to the house with me. We could get something cold to drink and sit down to read a book together. But now I can't take you with me because you screamed. I will have to leave you here with your mother so you will learn that when you scream to get your way, we will always do the opposite (rule #1)." Then turn and walk away. If she were to scream again, turn back and give her a spanking and then proceed to the house without her. If for some reason you are prevented from spanking (someone else's child, you are a foster parent, you are in a very public place, etc.), then just the denial of her desires will suffice to eventually stop the screaming—since it is the most necessary part of the training experience.

It is the principle of cause and effect; stimulus induced response; conditioned behavior. If a rabbit bumps against something in his cage and food falls in front of him, he will soon learn to repeat this behavior in order to reproduce the effect. If some response works for the child, she will keep trying it until she is sure it will no longer get the desired results. If you deny her the reward of getting her own way and then make the negative behavior painful, she will deny herself the screaming. ☺

Horse Sense

We have two horses that come to the back door and just stand around. I continually shoo them away—and clean my shoes. They have five acres of pasture, but they prefer the scraps that are thrown out to the dogs. What a dog will not eat is usually what a horse will eat. They love potato peelings and old cabbage, waiting hours for just one quick bite. Have you ever seen three dogs, five puppies and two horses trying to eat out of the same pan? Ten occasions of being slapped on the rear-end and chased down the hill to screams of "Wha horse!" does not deter them from coming up and scratching their flanks on my office window, waiting for a hand out. They think that getting screamed at and chased down the hill is part of the game of life. They live to gratify the flesh—no sense of self-control. They have been well trained to come to the back door.

You may wonder why I don't spend more time to train them properly. I confess that neither my dogs nor my horses are very well trained. I pay them little attention until they become intolerable. The truth is, I just don't care enough about them to spend the time needed. They just aren't worth the inconvenience. "He that hath ears to hear...." ☺

Epistles Epitomize Parental Performance

"Ye are our epistle written in our hearts, known and read of all men: Forasmuch as ye are manifestly declared to be the epistle of Christ ministered by us, written not with ink, but with the Spirit of the living God; not in tables of stone, but in fleshy tables of the heart (2 Corinthians 3:2-3)."

Paul characterized the Corinthians whom he had taught as a letter that all men could read. Paul's ministry was written in their every action. Likewise, our children are our epistles known and read of all men, hence our embarrassment when they are "publicly read." In high school, I did a sloppy job on a book report. When I was asked to read it publicly, I was ashamed because it revealed my shoddy efforts.

I have been in the presence of many families, and especially since we wrote To Train Up A Child, where the parents were nervously anxious about their children. It was obvious that they and the children were concerned about the children's performance. I could almost repeat verbatim the conversation they must have had in the car: "Now you better sit still and don't ask for anything and don't scuffle. Keep your feet off the furniture and sit still. Fold your hands in your lap and just sit there looking intelligent, or I will beat you to death when we leave. Do you understand me?" They were afraid their children were going to be "read" and the story would be unfavorable for the authors—the parents.

The zombie-eyed children file in and sit down like a Japanese delegation. I'm thinking, "What is wrong with these kids?" So I ask one of the more alert looking ones a question designed to provoke a little spark of humor: "Hey son (he is five years old), what do you do for a living?" He throws a concerned glance at his father whose eyebrows are screaming, "This better be good," and then says to me, "Oh I just obey my parents. It keeps me alive."

If you demand that your children perform better in public than in private, you are making the whole family into hypocrites. To be more concerned with public appearance than with real character is a statement that your reputation is your god. The children know this to be selfishness on your part. You are not building character in them, but deceit.

In the private moments, write on your children's hearts the things that are honest and pure, and you will not have to be concerned that someone will open the book to a censored chapter. An author of a book should never become angry with the contents. And he shouldn't write something he doesn't want made public. ☺

Consistency

A mother describes her dilemma: "I get so frustrated with the children. No matter how many times I tell them or spank them, they just do the same thing again. We just go around and around."

When a parent gives a command in a frenzied state of anger, the children take it seriously only as long as the parent is "hot." They interpret the parent's commands to be unreasonable and temporary, lasting only as long as the temper. If however, you give a solemn and forceful command when you are not at all emotionally wrought, the children assume that it is a well thought out command and not based on a temporary state of mind. When their disobedience does not upset you, but still meets with swift and sure penalty, they will believe they really are under new management. If, and *only* if, you are absolutely consistent, meeting every transgression with swift penalty, then they will quickly adapt themselves to the new order. They will do the incredible. They will obey.

You have tried everything else. How about trying consistency, 100% CONSISTENCY, every day, when it is inconvenient and when it is not, for their sakes and for yours? You need the rest. ☺

Plowing Under Weeds

Last week I was in Florida staying in the home of a young family. They had a thirty-month-old son that exemplified good training. He was a joy to be around. I was wondering how this young couple had managed to train him so well.

The next morning, I sat across the breakfast table from the mother as she was feeding her little eleven-month-old daughter. Suzy sat in the highchair reluctantly sucking down a spinach-squash-mush-mix, or some such concoction. It looked like barley green and egg yoke. I think I have discovered why some kids are so rebellious later in life. They are punishing their parents for what they were forced to eat when they were too young to know the difference and too small to resist.

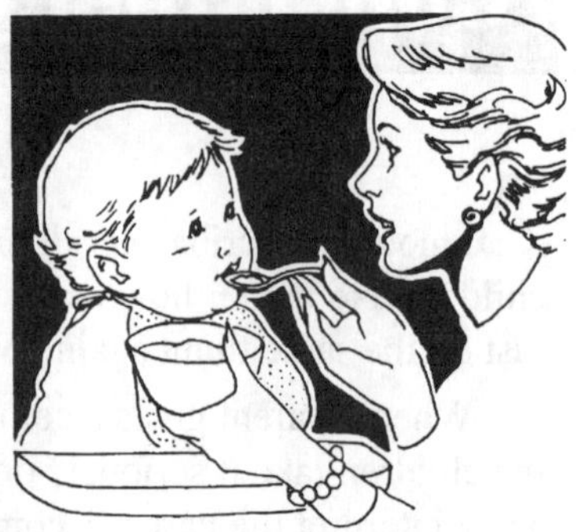

After about half of a jar, the little girl shoved it away. The mother pushed it back in front of her and said, "Don't you want some more, are you through?" Again the child shoved it away, this time with a little more force. It was one of those whole-body shoves, not violent, but determined. Her body language said, "I have had all of this I am going to tolerate. Get it out of my sight before I throw it in the floor." She didn't voice any protest other than a grunt, and she was not mean spirited. She was just practicing being independent, demonstrating her ability to enforce her rights.

Most mothers would have simply accepted the child's actions as a statement that she was through eating. However, this little mother was wise beyond her years. She picked up her little enforcer, which was lying on the table, and swatted the child's hand. When Mother once again placed the jar of green slime in front of Suzy, she tried to shove it away and received another spat. The mother spoke so quietly and so calmly that no one else at the table even noticed, "Suzy, are you through eating?" The little girl did not cry, but she got the message that she is not in control—Mother is. I could see that she wanted to push it away, but she looked at the little switch and restrained herself. Having conquered, the mother could have removed the tempting jar and continued her meal with no danger of interruption, but she left the jar sitting in front of the child during the rest of the meal to further enforce her victory. She didn't intend to feed the child any more; she just wanted to cement her authority. She was not going to allow the child to override her will in any way.

I watched the little girl stare at the jar, search her mother's face, and consider rejoining the battle. She would start to reach for the jar and then jerk her hand back as if it had been switched. Mother didn't appear to even be watching. The child was training herself! It took several minutes for her to relax and ignore the jar, but she never again touched it during the remainder of the meal.

I loved it. It was beautiful. It was the making of a well disciplined, self-controlled, balanced teenager. In that little girl's heart, the seeds of rebellion were just germinating. She was fomenting the sins of Lucifer: *"I will be like the Most High, I will ascend, I will exalt my throne... (Isa. 14:13-14)."*

The thing that makes it difficult for parents is that at such a young age the rebellion is so easy to overlook. At times it is even cute. "It doesn't hurt anyone; it is not inconvenient, embarrassing, or trying on our patience. We are not personally irritated, so why bother? Wait until it gets to be a problem." If a farmer waits until the little blades of grass get to be a problem, he has lost his crop. Before the roots get too deep, the farmer plows or cultivates out the grass. When more seeds germinate, and grass and weeds begin to grow, the farmer again plows it under. By dealing with the problem before it is a problem, it never becomes a problem.

Most parents wait until the weeds of self-will and indulgence are choking their children and disrupting the family before they try to pull them. The world and the Devil are always sowing tares in the flesh of our children. If we "sleep" and allow the weeds to get high enough to become visible, we might just have to "let them both grow together until the harvest, lest while ye gather up the tares, ye root up also the wheat with them."

There was a conflict in this eleven-month-old child. It was a tiny conflict, but it involved her whole soul. The tiny seeds seemed insignificant, but all deep-rooted weeds begin as harmless little sprigs. The character she will have as an adult was being formed over that jar of baby food. The way parents respond to the eleven-month-old is one-hundred times more important than how they respond to the fourteen-year-old. Tares that can be so easily pulled in a small child cannot be pulled at all in a teenager.

One year, I allowed grass to grow up around some bell pepper plants. I had cultivated out the center of the row and was proud of the way my garden looked. But I had neglected the grass that was growing immediately next to some of the plants, concealed by the foliage. When it finally came to my attention, I decided that I would pull it tomorrow. I got distracted, we had some good rains, the sun shone warm, and the grass roots entwined with the roots of the bell peppers. When the pepper plant started to bear fruit, the grass was then nearly as big as the pepper plant. I decided to pull the grass. You guessed it, the pepper plant was uprooted with the grass. I stood there holding my beautiful bell pepper plant feeling like a stupid sluggard. When I found weeds tangled in the roots of other plants, I let them both grow together. The fruit was greatly decreased, but at least I didn't kill the whole plant. I have seen parents "uproot" their older children in the process of trying to pull the tares that they allowed to mature. Pressured by parents who suddenly decide to clean house, some children totally rebel and run away from home—or commit suicide. This little mother did know, however, how to pull little tares from the flesh of her eleven-month-old daughter.

If you will take time to anticipate the character you desire in you teenagers and cultivate it while they are young, you will be able to enjoy the fruit later on. We gardeners know that it is much easier to weed early in the season, before the sun gets hot, and the ground gets hard. If you wait too long, you may wait until the experience is so painful and humiliating that you give up on one of your "plants" and say, "Well maybe next year—next child." It is sad to come to that place, but many of you are there right now.

I must encourage those of you with small children, train up your children now. Do not wait until they are one year old to start training. Rebellion and self-will should be broken in the six-month-old when it first appears. Take this young mother's example and think of ways you can train your child. ☺

Curriculum

Question: ***"What curriculum do you recommend for my six-year-old just starting school?"***

Do you have any change around the house? How about a tape measure? Raisins and M&M's are handy little math tools. Now you are set for Math Class for the next three or four years. I'm not being funny. So many parents spend money on expensive curriculum and forget that the reason we teach math is so little Sara will know how to make change, sew a dress, and total up her catalog order. Your question reveals that you have accepted some erroneous presuppositions.

You have been schooling your children since they were born. While shopping, driving down the road, or piddling around the house, have you taught them to recognize colors, shapes, numbers? Through looking at books with you, can they distinguish one animal from another? Do they know how many fingers they have on one hand, the total on both hands? Have they watched you cut up a chicken and discussed the body structure? Have you sat with them in the yard and examined bugs and worms? Have you looked at a globe to see how the world is arranged? Have they stacked blocks and balanced their weight on a seesaw? Have you corrected their grammar and taught them to write their names? Have you provided colors and paper for them to doodle? Well, they have already had biology 101, natural physics, general math, world geography, English grammar, art appreciation, and home economics.

But you feel a compulsion to do something that looks more like the school everyone is familiar with. You have accepted the pressure placed on you from the State and from friends and relatives. You are ready to stop being a parent and to become a teacher. The children are now going to suddenly become students. You feel you need something to validate your decision to homeschool, something tangible.

Remember, God did not make classroom education. It is the invention of humanists seeking to usurp parental authority. Why recapture your rights and duty only to adopt their methods of teaching? We are not talking about the material that is taught, but how it is taught. Classrooms are as unnatural as welding schools or boot camps. If an adult desires to enter into an occupational specialty, the classroom may be a pain that must be endured, but God save our children from the accountability and demands of professional students.

God has clearly defined the manner in which parents should teach: *"And thou shalt teach them diligently unto thy children, and shalt talk of them when thou sittest in thine house, and when thou walkest by the way, and when thou liest down, and when thou risest up. And thou shalt bind them for a sign upon thine hand, and they shall be as frontlets between thine eyes. And thou shalt write them upon the posts of thy house, and on thy gates. (Deuteronomy 6:7-9)."*

Maybe you could follow this rule: If a workbook can be enjoyed by the children, if they desire to do it just for fun, then it cannot be harmful unless they become so absorbed in books that they neglect the important social and work aspects of family. Except on rare occasions, book studies should never consume a large part of the day. Children should be engaged in work and play with their families. A young daughter needs to begin early learning and practicing to be a wife, mother, and home-keeper. A boy should begin early, two years old, practicing to be the man of the house and the President of the United States. He should be given responsibility and an important role in sustaining the family. Our first concern should be the development of character, work ethic, and personal confidence.

So many of you are needlessly worried about your ability to teach. In a society full of books, you can hardly keep a child from learning to read. There is no reading mother so ignorant that she will prevent her children from reading if she only encourages them.

But I have seen well educated, demanding mothers and professional teachers cause children to be so crushed in confidence or so bored to tears that they feared to even try to read. Forget the early achiever drive. Too many parents drive their children for their own satisfaction.

Primitive tribesman can be taught to read in one year. A ten or twelve-year-old American who has been exposed to letters and some phonics can learn to read in three months. But a child who fears failure will not even try. In a reading society, a child who wants to read will do so, regardless of the lack of formal teaching.

Relax, and then relax some more. Finally, relax with your children. Talk with them. Answer their questions about the why and how of everything. Have a good time discovering things together. Don't give them tests and scores. How would you like to have your teaching rated? Would you be encouraged in your endeavors, or would you feel like hiding for fear of failure? You might do some panic studying, but you would hate it. This is not what you want for your children. Take the pressure off. If need be, let them be two to four years behind the standard age level, and they will be far ahead by the time they are sixteen.

Some of you are so brainwashed, you don't believe this. We taught all five of our children in just this manner. When our oldest went off to college, she earned a four point average the first year. Most of our children did not learn to read until they were ten years old, but they all enjoy reading and are exceptionally good readers.

Understanding the principle of teaching *"while walking in the way (Deuteronomy 6:7-9)"* does not mean that you ignore teaching, but rather that you do it as a natural course of daily life. The children will not know they are in school; they will think you are just taking more interest in them, or that you have decided to have some fun with them rather than knock around like a frustrated commander fearing mutiny.

Everyday-life is your curriculum. It will be the place where your children will face their ultimate tests. It will be the ground on which they must apply what they have learned. Everyday-life is the best classroom and, with a little guidance, the best teacher. ☺

The Light of the Devil's Eye

Question: "Do you feel there is anything good on TV?"

I have seen several good things on TV. I once saw a family picture on the TV. It was sitting beside a set of good books.

Yes, the TV has some good programming, though I do not include the news and sports in that list. Particularly good are some of the educational programs. You can't believe everything they say, but it is a valuable viewpoint.

I have two concerns with the TV, however. One is the fact that it is impossible to have one around and search for the good stuff without eventually being exposed to the garbage. I would not dig through a garbage can of slop to find the one good biscuit lying in the bottom. Commercials are full of corruption, and even programs like *Little House on the Prairie* are strong on humanism.

The second problem I have with TV is that it is a thief. It robs the individual of time and creativity. Watching TV is a cessation of reality. It is an intoxicating withdrawal from the real world. The family with a TV is bucking the odds. The family without a TV stands a better chance of achieving righteous goals. Basically, watching Hollywood productions is an activity of the flesh, and can only produce carnality.

I hear a cry of legalism coming from the garbage can! OK, if you can pray the following prayer over the things you watch, then by all means watch them.

"Dear Lord, we invite you to come join us in this time of viewing. As your children, we commit this time to you as worthy of our attention. May our family be uplifted by this hour before the screen. And Lord, we pray that families everywhere would have the opportunity to do likewise. We thank you for providing this program for us, and we ask you to bless it to the edification of the Holy Spirit within. Now Lord, bless the men and women who produced this show and those who made it available us. May they have your blessings to do more of the same. In Jesus name, we thank you, Amen."

I challenge you to copy this prayer on a card, large enough to be seen from anywhere in the room, and place it over your TV for all who enter to read. Then have the whole family read it out loud before each viewing.

You can send your newsletter cancellations to the address on the back. ☹

Bad Attitude

In one of our recent seminars, a mother complained to Debi, "The children frustrate me so much. I tell them to do their schoolwork, and they just piddle around. I tell them to clean up their rooms, and they fuss over who is to clean up what. They are always irritating one another. It frustrates me so much, trying to cause them to maintain a good attitude. They are always complaining and whining about something. I get frustrated and spank them, but it seems to do no good. They just don't seem to care. They pick on each other continuously. I get so frustrated...." Debi interrupted her mournful complaints to answer, "Yes, it is an attitude problem." The weary mother hastily agreed, "That's it! They have bad attitudes." Debi responded, "No, it's you that has the bad attitude." The mother's widening eyes and gaping mouth expressed her dismay as she stood waiting for the forthcoming explanation.

Are you a frustrated parent? Is your brow drawn tight as if pulled by drawstrings? If parenting is not enjoyable, be assured, you have a bad attitude. When your children look into your face, what do they see? They are not fooled. They know how you feel toward them. Your face is a graph of approval or rejection. The smooth tongue of "positive affirmation" is not enough; in fact, it is worse than nothing if there is not genuine delight in your heart. Children can see through a parent who is made of muddy water. If they see disappointment and criticism, they will answer in kind. Discontented parents breed discontented children. Your attitude is the root of the family attitude tree. A bitter root cannot produce sweet fruit.

Parental attitudes are highly contagious, and children usually come down with a worse case. "More is caught than taught." And children seem more highly susceptible to catching a bad attitude than of being taught to have a good one. They can catch the disease of bad attitude while being passive. On the other hand, they must exert themselves to have a good attitude.

"Our actions speak louder than our words," but our attitude screams louder than our actions. The first need and the most lacking element in child training is a right attitude on the part of parents. You may say, "I have a good attitude, I am just too busy." When you have all these obligations to fulfill and the children make demands on you, how do you feel toward them? That's an attitude. If our motive or our attitude is wrong, our technique can never be right. Who you are is more important than what you do.

Your children are playing follow-the-leader. They are deaf to your words, but they "hear" your attitude loud and clear. Example has always been more effective than theory. Where parents are constantly modeling the bad attitude; a good attitude is just a theoretical concept to the children. Try as they may, they can't quite fathom the meaning of a good attitude—it has been so long since they have seen one. If you dress your children in tight pinching shoes, don't blame them for having sore feet.

The bad news is that you are responsible for the condition of your children. The good news is that you don't have to be frustrated over attempting to change them. You only need to change yourself. Since their attitudes are reflections of your own, you need only change your attitude, and the reflections will change.

I know you are only expressing your displeasure over their foolishness. You are using your disapproving scowl as a threat to induce them to shame. They are supposed to so crave your approval that they make great sacrifices to win your smile. It isn't working, is it? Actually, you are working against the very thing you desire to achieve.

There is a natural principle you must understand: Children living under condemnation are not motivated to good works. None of us seeks to please someone who is condemning us. You have trained your face to display a nearly constant look of disapproval, disappointment, and frustration. You may nag or gripe them into relenting to your will, but you can never bad-attitude them into a good attitude. Children cannot be intimidated into positive character. To stand off and criticize their performance will not induce them to a rectifying shame. No one has ever been motivated to climb out from under a pile of disapproval to win the praise and affections of his or her accuser.

The law of human nature is such that condemnation and shame cause an alienation that only produces more disobedience. Paul said, *"The motions of sins, which were by the law, did work in our members to bring forth fruit unto death (Romans 7:5)." "Because the law worketh wrath... (Romans 4:15)."* But if you become so disappointed with their failure that you assume an air of judicial condemnation, they will unwillingly accept the blame, but THEY WILL NOT HAVE THE MORAL COURAGE TO CHANGE. Law and condemnation never produce righteousness. If you are always ready to show them what is wrong, but do not constantly exemplify what is right, they will cower under your judgments while continuing to grow into the likeness of your graceless bitterness.

The parental spirit of displeasure holds the child in "death." A new spirit in the parent will allow the child to serve from a joyous spirit and not from the decrepit bondage of legal depression. In our relationship to God, it is called *"newness of spirit."* *"But now we are delivered from the law, that being dead wherein we were held; that we should serve in newness of spirit, and not in the oldness of the letter (Romans 7:5-6)."*

Mother, if every time you looked at your husband you saw his dissatisfaction and disappointment, if he sighed with defeat over what a lousy wife you are, would you feel inspired to make improvements? Absolutely not! You would withdraw. If your are spunky in spirit, you might fight back and give him further reason for rejection, but if you are broken in spirit, you would quietly withdraw. You would then seek friendship and approval elsewhere.

Your children will begin to develop positive character only in an atmosphere of forgiveness and acceptance. The first step to recovery and the ground on which it continues is the parent's smile. In our book, To Train Up A Child, we have a chapter called Tying Strings. Parent, you need to tie strings of fellowship through your smiles, strings of trust through a display of trust, strings of respect through mutual respect, strings of kindness, grace, and forgiveness. You can not disapprove your children into heart compliance, but you can example them in, smile them in, care them in, patience them in, and woo them in with a heart that exemplifies Christlike character.

If *"the joy of the Lord is our strength,"* then surely the joy of the parents is the strength of a child. If fellowship with God provokes His children to holiness, what will be the result of a child's fellowship with his parents? The best training is done under the supervision of a smile. There is a time for discipline, rebuke, spanking, and even controlled anger, but such should be temporary signposts on a path of communion that you walk with your children. If they see your delight and appreciation, they will have the courage to try to maintain that sweetness.

Parent, relax. Lay back. Slow down. Enjoy the trip. If you can't train your children to meet your high standards, lower the standards until they can reach them. We are not talking about the law of God. We are talking about muddy feet, carrying out the garbage, picking up dirty clothes, doing schoolwork, etc. Put the bar low enough so that with the effort they are willing to give, they can clear the hurtle and finish each day a winner. Raise the bar a little at a time so they can improve but will always be a winner.

When we are dealing with emotionally crippled children, this is even more important. We must cast out our concepts of what they are *able* to do and ask ourselves what they are *willing* to do. What level of performance can we realistically hope to achieve? There is more than one kind of incapacity. It is hard for parents to admit that their child is hurt, broken, and enslaved to a front of indifference and bitterness. If you set the standard beyond their willing efforts, you will cause them to cease trying. They will be like the kid in public school who is already behind two years. He cares so much that, to keep from being further hurt, he pretends not to care at all. He is just killing time until he gets old enough to quit. You don't have much longer. They grow up fast. Hold that soul with compassion and understanding. Be a friend. Show mercy. Smile. ☺

Mistraining at Three Months

One of the young mothers in the church tells how she trained her three-month-old daughter to cry and whine to be picked up and held. Upon seeing her parents start to drift into another room, the baby cried out. The father responded, "Get little Suzy, she wants to be with us." Mother picked up Suzy, and she spread her beautiful smile in delight. Well, that's the real life story of how Suzy was trained to whine. She initiated an act, whining, to which the mother responded by picking her up. That was the first day of a lifelong habit.

She will refine her technique, employing more threats and spreading more misery. She will eventually fall on the floor, kicking her feet and screaming. The mother will be embarrassed in public, frustrated and angry at home, and will eventually have such contention and strife between her and her demanding daughter that she will write a letter to us wanting to know how to deal with an angry, undisciplined and unthankful teenager.

At less than three months old this little girl had discovered the power of emotional manipulation. For several days she refined her technique of control. She discovered how to use her mother's guilt against her. She is so sweet, such a delight—as long as she is getting her way. Most parents will tolerate this behavior until the child is a two-year-old terror, and then they will decide that maybe she is about old enough to start getting a spanking for her fits. The first good spanking will produce the greatest tantrum yet, and the parents will decide that their child just has a double dose of that "sinful nature" they heard the preacher talking about. When the little girl is taken to the professionals, they will tag her with the Attention Deficit Disorder lie.

But the story didn't end there. This wise mother decided to retrain her three-month-old baby. She laid her down, knowing she would cry, then calmly ignored her crying. When Suzy stopped crying and became cheerful, Mother picked her up and played with her. When Suzy was placed in the crib and again cried, the mother again ignored her until she became cheerful. Through a several day process of never paying her any attention when she cried, Suzy stopped crying to get her way. Now, four-month-old Suzy never cries to get her way. Why go to the trouble if it doesn't work? She is trained to maintain a good attitude. This training has extended to every area of Suzy's life.

I hear a frustrated mother of five- and six-year-olds saying, "Yea, but wait till they get older!" Suzy's mother has older children who are well trained, being cheerful and obedient in all things. She started being faithful about two years ago, and it has paid off. I heard this mother say, "It's so fun training my children; I enjoy them so much!"

A few days later, a fifteen-year-old girl was visiting and Suzy's mother said, "Pick up Suzy and hold her a while." The teenager responded, "Why? She isn't crying." The mother explained, "I never pick her up when she is crying because she will then be trained to always cry to get her way. Rather, I reward her good behavior." The teenager immediately saw the wisdom of her methods. Maybe when this young girl becomes a mother she will have the wisdom to begin training her newborns and not wait until they are three months old. ☺

Volley Ball No Bawler?

This past fall on the volleyball court another episode in the ongoing saga of child training was played out on a nearby pallet where a mother daily deposited her crying nine-month-old daughter. Every afternoon when we played volleyball, the parents would take turns sitting out of the game and entertaining the little griper. This is their first child and they are both good parents. They thought it was their duty to meet their daughter's "emotional" needs. You wouldn't be a good parent to let your poor child sit on the pallet alone and cry—would you?

You can't imagine how hard it is to keep your mouth shut sometimes. Well, this was one of those times when I didn't. I finally blurted out, "Why don't you just let her cry? If you don't go to her, she will learn to entertain herself." Several days later I noticed that the child was sitting alone without crying. When a friend started to go to the little girl, the mother warned her saying, "Don't go to her, when you leave she will start crying." Again I butted in, suggesting that the mother do precisely that: Every ten minutes go to the cheerful child and pat her on the head. When you walk off she may cry, but she will see that the crying will not prevent you from leaving. Over a two hour period you will continually reinforce your indifference to her demanding whine.

In just a few days the little girl was content to play alone and to receive periodic attention without crying to manipulate others into servitude. Today she is the most cheerful and happy baby around. Her mother is as proud as a young hen with a double yoke egg. ☺

Training Teens?

Dear Michael

I have a fourteen-year-old son who is worldly-minded. He gets his hair cut so that his bangs hang down over his eye on one side. He will sit in church and sort of swing his head so that his bangs bounce around. It appears that he likes to peek at the world through his pretty hair. It seems that he becomes totally absorbed with how he looks. It is embarrassing and, I am ashamed to admit it, but sometimes when I look at him I am disgusted. He is not satisfied with his clothes or shoes unless they are the current fashion. When I tell him how ridiculous he looks, he only withdraws. When I try to curb his desires for the latest fashions, he becomes miserable until we give him what he wants.

I don't want him to be unpopular or rejected because of his clothes. He doesn't get along with his brothers and sister but has friends he would rather be with. I know that we have made some mistakes, but what can we do to correct the situation? It seems we have lost touch with him. It is as if we are in two different worlds. We do not want to drive the wedge deeper.

His father doesn't say much. He is always busy working and doesn't seem to notice what is going on. I know that my son is not going to change as long as I have a critical spirit toward him. I am desperate. Do you have any suggestions on how to retrain him?

Sincerely,

Any One of a Thousand

"Groannnnn." That's the sound I make sitting at my desk trying to answer a letter like this. I feel like the station attendant when the lady drives the car in on a flapping, fragmented, flat tire and then wants him to fix it. "Lady, it should have been fixed back down the road where the flat first occurred."

There is something you must understand about yourself and your child. There is a strange struggle, a competition, taking place. Your relationship to this child began in infancy with him totally dependent. As he grew older, your words could move and persuade him. Your logic was beyond assail, your power omnipotent. You were loved, feared, and respected. He began as a young sapling that could be bent to your will, caused to grow in any direction. You took your control for granted. You didn't see the curve of independence asserting itself in the relationship.

Suddenly you find your dependent child has become stiff and unyielding with a mind and will of his own. He disdains your logic. Your reasons are without foundation. You don't understand him. You are old-fashioned, out of touch. He views you as one who is trying to persecute him and keep him from happiness. He alone has experienced the passions and joys of life. He is ready to feel, taste and experience. He stands on the edge of the great thrill of life, and you, with all your talk of duty and responsibility, you are the enemy. His friends "understand him" because they are in the same passionate vortex. It has never dawned on him that you weren't born a hardened adult. He doesn't know that you once had the same disease called *youth* and got over it.

A child is kneadable clay, still being formed, but an adult is pottery baked in the oven of time. Between the trainable child and the unyielding adult is the twelve to sixteen-year-old, the adolescent. They are like clay, half baked in the sun. It is too late to forcibly remold them, but they are not yet so hardened as to be totally beyond reclaiming. The twelve-year-olds may demand the independence and liberty of adults, while having the emotional needs of small children. The adolescents expect the security of being mothered and the supremacy of being adults. Their struggles come because they possess the developing passions of an adult with the self-indulgent mentality of a child. They have always lived by their wants. Their unrestrained indulgences appeared to be no problem when the consequences were nothing more than unmade beds, chewing gum in their hair, and cavities. But an unrestrained teenager can reap terribly bitter fruit.

It is natural for children to grow into a state of independence, to gradually assume the command of their lives. It is when they demonstrate ineptness of responsibility that we parents become upset. It is not a question of giving them independence, they most certainly grow into it. We parents enjoy handing the reins to the children and saying, “You can drive awhile.” But the day comes when they do not drive as we think they should. When we demand they give over the reins, we find ourselves looking into the determined, independent face of a twelve to sixteen-year-old adult. They are forever beyond being governed from without. It is a hard adjustment for the parents to make, for the young teen wants to be fed and protected in the nest, but wants to wander without accountability.

We parents know our children are making bad decisions, but when we try to intervene they are resentful. We see them eating our food and greedily demanding more of the luxuries our money can buy, but unwilling to accept our jurisdiction over their lifestyles. Young teenagers are no more on their own than when they were three, but they demand that everyone respect their rights to sovereignty. We figure that with the food and clothes we provide and the roof we keep over their heads we have purchased the right to govern. But, having spent their entire lives totally cared for, they continue to feel it is their due. So parents and older children don’t see the world through the same glasses. Our wisdom and judgment has always overruled their opinions. They turn twelve or fourteen and suddenly we have lost all persuasive powers.

If a child turns eighteen and walks away to provide his own roof, food, clothes, etc., we can readily relinquish our hold; but a totally dependent fourteen-year-old, suddenly assuming that he is wiser than we are, is hard to swallow, especially when his hand is still in our pockets.

We parents have great aspirations for our children. We want the best for them. We have made mistakes and have witnessed the mistakes of others. We know where the pitfalls and deathtraps are located, and it is hard to see our children blinded, arrogantly rushing across a battlefield where we have seen many casualties fall, some to never rise again.

So it is in this betwixt-and-between stage that parents are uncomfortable with the child's growing independence, and the child is uncomfortable with the parents' clinging governorship. Ideally, the parent should have prepared the child to be responsible in his growing independence. We should be training them toward the time when they will make decisions alone. It is a joy to see your child wisely assume command of his own life. It is comforting to relinquish your authority when you can trust the hands that receive it. But to see an irresponsible child destroy all that you thought you were building is misery indeed. To have him or her rebel and run helter-skelter into sure destruction is the ultimate disappointment in life.

So in answer to the original question: "What can I do to train my fourteen-year-old son?" IT IS TOO LATE TO TRAIN HIM. He is beyond the powerplays and the unquestioning submission. He is no longer one of the "little children" to whom the kingdom of God belongs. He is a skeptic where your opinions are concerned. He sees your hypocrisy and will not respect anyone who is not respectable. He will give no honor based on rank. He is a free moral agent, bent on demonstrating his independence.

You must change your approach from hot demands to respectful persuasion. It is too late to forcibly cut his hair. Too late to make demands without good logic behind it. As an independent free agent he must be persuaded. His own will, based on his own values, will be the ruling factor in his life. You must win his confidence and earn a right to be his counselor. Your anger that once caused him to cower and submit will now only cause him to withdraw. There was a time when demonstrating how hurt you were broke his heart and made him submit. Today it disgusts him and makes him seek friendships elsewhere.

However, you should not let guilt over your failure cause you to submit to your teenager's tyranny. You should take authority over your house and all who live in it. You are the proprietor of your property. You can no longer tell your "tenants" how to think, but you still have sovereign control over all your assets. Your child's soul may have grown out from under your jurisdiction, but as long as he is under your roof, eating your food, his actions are still under your control. You must earn the right to enter his soul, but he should be made to understand that he must earn the right to live in your house and eat your food. Where a teenager will resent your jurisdiction over his soul, he will respect your right and authority over the outward management of your home and resources. If you are dignified and calm in your legislation, he will respect it, even if he gripes. For instance: You do not have to pay for designer clothes. You should provide modest clothes that are serviceable, nothing more. You don't have to give him any allowance at all. He can work for it. You need not pick up after him and cater to his wants. You have a right to control the music and TV in your house, if you have such. He will expect you to exercise control over all physical and external matters of running a smooth household. He will appreciate your demands that he treat every member of the house with the same respect that you do.

Of course, if you are a screaming idiot, he will not respect your rebuke for his tantrums. If you are indulgent, your demands that he not be indulgent will only be met with ridicule. If you are worldly in your approach to dress, he will show no honor when you want him to dress modestly and practically.

Parents, how did your children get in their present condition? They were not born that way. How did they learn about designer clothes and mod hair cuts? How did they develop associations with worldly kids? You didn't send them to the public or private school, but did you put them in a position to be part of a youth group in a large public church? Did you take them shopping in the malls? Do you coo over chic clothing styles? If your children are trying to conform to the world instead of being transformed by the renewing of their minds, it is because you have provided a worldly environment to allure them. If they act like some of the jerk comedians on the TV, is it is because they admire someone whom you once thought was funny? If they have an "I could't care less" attitude, perhaps they learned it from Hollywood. If you cause a pumpkin to grow hanging on a fence, you should expect it to have impressions of the wire on its outer skin. Though it is not the final deciding factor, the environment is the mold in which your child is formed. While you gave no particular concern to training, their world was a constant training ground.

Yet now you cry out with a broken heart. You are willing to take the blame. You are willing to correct those faults in your own character. You are willing to purge your home and environment of worldly influence. But what can you do to rectify the wrong? **You can start by becoming the person you desire your child to be.** No double-mindedness or two-faced frauds. You must be a real Christian through and through. To have a little revival in your child's soul, you must have a big one in your own. They can not be changed by you from without, but they can be changed by themselves and God from within. Your job is to *lead* them TO DESIRE goodness with all their hearts. You can not push with criticism. You must LEAD THEM by example.

Understand your limitations and your authority. You have the authority to rule the home and everyone in it, externally. But, in dealing with your teenager's soul, you are limited to PERSUASION and counsel based on mutual respect. You can tell them what to do in regard to the family environment, but you cannot tell them how to feel. You can teach and *exemplify* values, but you cannot *legislate* values.

For a teenager it is too late to "train up a child," but it is not too late to lead them into the paths of righteousness. Instead of standing behind your children and trying to criticize them in the right direction, rise up in the beauty of holiness and invite them to join you. ☺

Potty Training at Three Months

My name is Susanna Beachy. I am a thirty-year-old mother of three children. I didn't potty train my first two babies until they were walking, but when the third one came along the Pearls came over one day when my little girl was just two months old. Mike and Deb asked, "Why aren't you potty training this child?" I looked at my tiny, squirming girl and said, "Can it really be done? Is it possible?" I didn't believe it, but I knew the Pearls didn't lie, so I asked them to tell me how it was done.

Well, after careful instruction, I tried it. It was harder training me than it was training my infant. For the first week I kept her in cloth diapers and maintained close contact. I held her nearly all the time or kept her sitting close enough where I could keep a hand or foot on her cloth diaper. When I felt the diaper grow warm from wetting, I make a sound like running water— "sssssss." By the end of the third day, to my daughter, "sssssss" meant it is time to pee-pee. When I suspected that it was about time for a wetting, I would make the sound and she would respond by wetting. Her "let down" was automatic. She never even knew she was being conditioned. When I started putting her on a little child's potty, the added cold on her bottom became an additional cue to respond with a wetting.

I kept this up for about a month, even though it was time consuming. I had success most of the time, but there were times when she would still go in her diaper. I thought I was failing until I went back and talked to Mama Deb [very local endearment only]. She explained that the idea of early potty training was not to achieve perfect results, but to communicate to the child that going on the pot was the natural and normal thing to do.

My four-month-old is comfortable going on the potty. It is natural to her. She knows what I expect of her when I sit her on it and make the appropriate sound. By the time she is walking, I expect her to be taking herself to the toilet.

If you train them to think that going in their pants is natural, then when they are older and you suddenly start putting them on the cold, unfriendly toilet, you can not expect it to cause a "let down."

I would encourage you other mothers: Don't let this become another pressure on you. It is a lot better for the children to have a relaxed, contented mother than it is for you to potty train the baby. I don't let this be stressful to me. I only take the baby when I go or whenever it is apparent that she needs to go. I don't push myself or the baby. If the baby gets red in the face or gets a still, concentrating look on her face, I know she is going to relieve herself. Once you become aware of your baby's cycle, it is not hard to catch it. I use Pampers with Velcro, and a diaper will often last all day if I am careful. It saves a lot of diapers, and it is bringing my baby up with the right idea.

I think, if it is possible, it has made my baby even more precious to me through the extra time I have spent with her. When everything goes off right and she looks up into my face with a satisfied little smile, it is worth every moment. ☺

Preparation

Children study certain subjects to prepare for a medical career; why not teach your little ones to think of the day when God can use them to go to a field that is white unto harvest. Their geography class may entail following the work and needs of the missionaries on a world map. Their math class can be collecting castoff items from other families, having a garage sale, counting the money, learning how to get a money order, and sending it to a missionary. Their language class could be writing missionaries to tell them you have marked their position on the map and are praying for them. Give your children a vision—God's vision of reaching every tongue, kindred and nation.

Kids simply need to be asked regularly, "So what are you going to do with this life God has given you?" Whether the answer is towards ministry or some other occupation, it will at least break the trance that seems to grip youngsters. ☺

The Five-year-old Whine baby

My daughter Shalom came home telling the following experience. I told her to go write it down. This is the view of a fourteen-year-old in her own words:

My friend and I returned from the store with ice cream. When we met her little brother and sister and gave them some ice cream, he just whined as usual. He always wants something different from what you give him. But his older sister usually just says, "No, eat that one," or sometimes she gives him hers. This little boy whines about a lot of stuff to get his way.

Later that afternoon, my friend was giving coffee to her daddy and the little boy whined for some as well. But after several times of whining and her saying "No," he finally gave up and started whining for hot chocolate. When the sister said "No," again he continued to whine. She kept saying, "You can have water but no coffee or chocolate." By this time I could see that they were training him into a whine baby, so I said, "No, he can't have water either, if he is going to whine for it." He went into the corner and pouted at me for not giving in to his whining.

I explained to the sister that when he whined for a different ice-cream bar, I would not give him any ice-cream at all. After three times he would be happy with what he got.

When whining for coffee or hot chocolate, instead of rewarding him with water, I would say, "No water for an hour or until we eat dinner." Do not reward whining, no matter what happens. ☺

A wise son maketh a glad father: but a foolish son *is* the heaviness of his mother. Proverbs 10:1

Pubermania

Mother number one: "I simply can't understand what has happen to my son John. He has always been the one child I could trust to consistently do what is right. He has always been so thoughtful, polite and sensitive to the younger children; and even though his attitude is still good, he does the most unexpectedly mean things. Like the other day, I heard his younger brothers crying and hollering. I raced into the room and found him sitting on them, holding one in a headlock and laughing, having a great time. He was ashamed as soon as I began to reprimand him, and he immediately asked his little brothers to forgive him. How could he enjoy doing something so mean and then have such a repentant heart five minutes later? What has happened to my son?"

Mother number one thousand, three hundred and seventy two: "Our thirteen-year-old son has always been such a joy to us. He has a heart for God that has caused him to seek to do all he can for others. But just lately, totally out of character, he seems to be asserting his will over mine. It's like he wants to gain authority over his younger brothers and sisters and occasionally, even me. This new person really runs into trouble with his father, who takes his son's questions as a personal insult and really comes down hard. For the first time as parents, we disagree on how to handle our children. We both know we cannot let it go, but how do we deal with this new kid? Our son's attitude still seems so right, but it almost looks like a seed of rebellion. It is hard to explain. What has happened to my sweet little boy?"

Debi Pearl responds:

Have you ever raised chickens? We have eight hens and one rooster. Many times I have gone out to work in the garden and noticed our rooster making a pest of himself. The hens will be busy scratching the ground, and then he runs over and shoves them away. The little hens just turn and start scratching some other place. The rooster waits a few seconds and again shoves another one around. Of course, every time I open the hen house door I run for dear life, or he will be trying to shove me around. That crazy old rooster doesn't know how many times I have pondered putting him in the cooking pot. When Mike is outside, the rooster steers a wide path. On occasions Mike has had me let the hens out while he hides around the corner just so he can give the rooster a heart attack. I figure it takes a bigger rooster to intimidate a smaller rooster—and of course, enjoy the intimidation. It is a mystery to me why the rooster feels compelled to be such a jerk, but Mike thinks its real funny.

I said all this to tell you, I suspect your little roosters are feeling their natural hormonal competitive instincts, and as of yet haven't learned to harness their urges to dominate. Since it takes a rooster to understand a rooster, I'm going to let the big rooster in this family tell you how we handled this new and exciting challenge when our boys came of age.

Thanks for that introduction, Deb. Remember, behind every good rooster is a good hen. The two mothers above, voicing their concerns, are representative of many homeschool mothers. If your children are away from home most of the day, attending school, you will not be as aware of this change that occurs in the thirteen and fourteen-year-old boys. But when the mother has her "sweet son" under her constant tutelage, the inevitable physical and psychological changes that come with puberty will be a shock to her concept of childhood submission. The boy's "problem" is a result of gushing, exploding, rampaging hormones. In the Eastern cultures, it has been traditional to remove the boys from the women's quarters to the men's domain before this change takes place.

It is often obscured in our perverted culture, but a boy's destiny is to become a man. Although, prior to puberty, boys are psychologically different from girls, the contrast increases to stark dimensions when they each go through this natural, maturing change we call puberty. The male becomes more independent and domineering. This independence is not just directed at females but at all people and things. Keep in mind that the boys are growing into a role of leadership. Leadership in the male population is not just an office they inherit upon marriage or at some manhood graduation ceremony; it is a growing process that causes them to begin to assume authority at puberty. It is not natural for a woman to rule over a man. For that reason, the young man's conflict is more prominent with his mother than with his father.

You may observe, and want to protest, that your young teenage son is just a child with no abilities or wisdom to lead. This is generally true; but leadership in a man does not necessarily come from wisdom or ability. It is initially hormonal and psychological. The boys will become more competitive and aggressive. They begin to step away from the crowd (including the family) and seek their identity alone. They become self-assured and cocky. They are ready to conquer, go to war if necessary. As their "own man" they may question untried authority or challenge unproved regulations. They are beginning the process of marching to their own drumbeat, and not that of the crowd, including their mother's.

Fathers can also have a problem with this development in their sons. Remember, the father has been the rooster of the yard, and suddenly he is challenged. If he is insecure, especially if he does not have the submission of his wife, he may rise in anger against this challenging upstart. For twelve or thirteen years, with just a hard look he has been able to crush any challenge. Suddenly his hard look is returned. He may fly into a rage to try to strike down his challenger.

To compound the problem, if the father does not cherish the females in his life, the son may not discipline his own feelings of dominance or conquest. He must have his impulses tempered with wisdom and kindness. It is not desirable to break these male impulses, only to channel them. Gentlemen are not broken men who have no urges to conquer, but men who know how to vent their steam on creative living rather than against others. When a man or boy finds his identity in the process of ruling over others, it is an unjustified use of his impulses and powers.

When a young man (going through puberty) experiences this change, it is time for him to be engaged in hard work with the men. It is against nature to place a developing young man in the care of his mother. His impulses are to care for her. He needs to be straining his muscles, putting his back to the burden. If his education continues, it should be under the tutelage of the men. A boy could sit down for a short time to the teaching of his mother if his body and mind have been engaged in a man's world. The conflict comes when the parents do not recognize and provide outlets for his development. A little steam continuously released is of no consequence; but if it is bottled up, it will become a great explosion.

Ideally, the boys should be engaged in physical labor, but if you find yourself locked into this strange American culture and feel you are unable to make a change, understanding your son's developing passions will enable you to artificially make allowances. For instance, Mother, if you must have your son under your constant care, provide outdoor activity for him. Allow him to go out and do something physical about every hour. Do not try to pen him up like a docile female. Let the boys run, jump, holler, wrestle, climb, and race on bicycles. One mother supplied their garage with tools and had someone teach her boys how to use them. They spend most of their day making things, which they sell. When it does come time for book learning, they are calm and relaxed.

Some families have been able to create a mini farm on one or two acres where the boys can tend animals and make repairs or modifications on buildings or fences. Small engine repair or rebuilding old bicycles and selling them are just a few of the possibilities.

You say, "But my son is so ignorant now, he needs to be in school." Most of the boy's time is probably spent daydreaming and griping. Put him to a physically exhausting or mentally challenging task and he will learn more in one tenth of the classroom time.

Mother, you must turn loose of the sweet boy and let the man emerge. Demand respect and obedience, but learn to live with another man in the house. In the dark ages, they often castrated the male household servants to maintain the docile boys, living in unquestioning submission. I wouldn't give a dime for a boy who didn't put his brothers in a headlock occasionally. Real boys are like the old coal-burning steam engines; they make a lot of noise and smoke. They blow their whistles so everyone will know they are coming and get out of the way; but mostly they are just letting off steam. Mother, picture yourself as rearing a leader of other men, a conqueror of frontiers, a missionary who will laugh in the face of death and charge hell with a King James Bible; then you will not be disturbed by this growing change. ☺

Coming Out

I just returned from doing seminars in North Carolina. I had very pleasant stays in three different homes where each family had several children under eight years old. It is a renewing experience to interact with God-centered homeschooling families. I am encouraged by what I am seeing and the letters and reports I am receiving from all over the world. There is a slow, steady revival of holiness and deliverance. For the last fifty years, Satan has been increasingly trampling the homes of America into the mud. When it seemed that the children would be forsaken, wounded in the field, when it appeared parents had relinquished their duty to nurture their own children, when Hollywood was gobbling up the last bit of sanity left in the home, many of us had given up hope and retreated to a quiet place, thinking ourselves to be the last survivors of Christianity. But like the animals God called to Noah's ark, thousands were hearing a call to "Come out of her my people, that ye be not partakers of her sins (Rev. 18:4)."

I daily receive scores of letters, many telling of great victories in the home. God does indeed have His remnant. The scales of blindness are falling away and old-fashioned holiness is making a comeback. This is not a movement under one ministry or one denomination. In fact, I know of few churches that are even able to comprehend this phenomenon. We receive many letters from parents who are concerned because their church is the only remaining corrupting influence on their families. God is doing a work from the heart out, instead of from the pulpit down.

I encourage Bible believing pastors to wake up and clean out a corner in the church to contain this movement of God. It will not go away, but many families are leaving structured Christianity to gather in a protected environment with like-minded families. Our larger cities are dotted with hundreds of home churches. If the cream leaves our churches, pastors will become missionaries to what is left of their congregations.

Once Christian fathers and mothers muster the courage to stand up and take charge of their own lives, there is no stopping them from complete reformation of their families. The reform is personal, as seen by a change in diet, entertainment, and personal habits. The reform is economical, as seen by a movement to live debt free, below one's means rather than right on the edge. The reform is family centered, as seen by the increased size of the families and the structuring of time and activities around the family's needs. The reform is religious, as seen by the increase in personal and family devotion and holiness. The reform is medical, as seen by a revival of interest in herbs, natural childbirth, and personally taking charge of one's own diagnoses and treatment.

The reform is often occupational. Many fathers are moving their families out of the cities and into a simpler lifestyle. More fathers are seen with a hoe in their hands rather than golf clubs, and their children by their side rather than business associates. Mothers are seen standing with their girls, wearing aprons smudged with wheat flour, rather than standing in the shopping malls.

This is a revival of family life, of the Christian home. From these homes, as from a honey tree, flows a sweetness and purity that is a joy to see. I am thankful to live in this age and to be a part of this remnant of reform.

My prayer is that in our zeal to flee the world we do not become self-centered and withdrawn from those in need. As we choose our school, church, occupation, and neighbors, let us not become like the Pharisee who, seeking to justify himself, said, "Who is my neighbor?" If we clutch to ourselves the goodness of this movement, it will rot like the manna that fell daily in the wilderness. To minister to Christ is to minister to those in need. A ministering family is a growing family. A self-centered family is like a plant feeding upon it's own foliage. It will wither and die. By giving we receive. You will increase your family by tending to the dying of this world. Let us not save this great bounty for ourselves, but rather lead our children in giving it away. ☺

True Confessions of a Bed Wetter

Many of you have written us about the problem of your older children wetting their beds. Through our extensive social outreach we have persuaded one of these tormented souls to go public with her confession. You will read in her very own words the chronicle of her bitter struggle to rise above domestic shame and a wet mattress.

"When I was growing up I wet on the bed. I hated wetting on the bed and would have done anything to be able to stop. I played hard and I slept hard. I simply could not wake up! No amount of medication, discipline, or shaming could change my

personality. Today, I still run the day's course like the roadrunner himself. At night I sleep like the dead. Thankfully, when I was nine years old, my bladder finally learned to adjust.

My mom was a very practical woman. Every night she simply provided me with an old towel to stuff in my underpants, and she brought clean sheets every morning. The heavy-duty rubber cover protected the mattress, while my mother protected our secret.

To my shame, I never could spend the night away or go to camp without dread of wetting the bed.

But mom—bless her heart—never added to my shame. She made it as easy as possible on me until nature allowed relief.

To the many hundreds of moms who have written, I just want to say, "Relax," teach your bedwetting children to privately put on a towel or diaper at night. Remind them to go to the bathroom, but don't make an issue of it. They hate their problem more than you do. They are the ones who wake up cold, wet, smelly, and embarrassed.

Just like some kids learn to walk late, others need time to grow out of this problem. Remember, someday your child may grow up and write an article on bedwetting, or co-author a book on child training; so make sure you leave a good impression. This has been the confession of Debi Pearl. I do feel better now. ☺

Rights are Right

We receive many letters and public inquiries on the issue of personal rights. A mother asks, *"How can I teach my children to share? How can I teach them to play together without fighting over toys? They are constantly coming to me whining that someone has taken something away from them. I try to teach them they should share and be kind, but they seem to like fighting better. I get so frustrated I don't know what to do. I hate to admit it, but sometimes I just want to get away from them. I can't stand all the bickering."*

Another mother says: *"I have two boys, one eight and one ten. My daughters are five and two. The boys are always teasing their sisters. Anytime the girls go in the boys' room or play with anything that belongs to the boys, the boys become very selfish. They will not let their sisters play with them and are constantly running off and making them cry. I know that there is an age difference and that the boys and girls have different interests, but how can I teach the boys to give up their rights? They are not gentlemen and are sometimes just mean to their sisters. Is this a stage they will grow out of, or should I start spanking them more?"*

In Answer:

I can see a frustrated, harrowed mother as she takes a deep breath and tells herself not to get angry. The children are closing in from every side screaming, "Mother, make him play with me. Mother, he took my teddy bear away. She's sitting in my chair. I had it first. It's mine, give it to me!" So she sighs and once more adorns her arbitrators gown, taking the stand to hear the pros and cons from the accusing and excusing parties. She is never quite sure she has judged fairly, and most of the children are sure she hasn't. An appropriate family Bible verse becomes: *"There is no peace saith my God to the wicked."* She is privately convinced she has the most unchristian four- and six-year-olds in the Western world.

When our children begin to demand their own way and practice the "me first" philosophy, we know it is a root of sin manifesting itself. So we referee apart the clenched competitors and demand they give over their rights. In futility, we sing the give-over song to the beat of their exchanged blows. And all our sincere warnings against selfishness are punctuated by screams and protests of unfairness.

Your legislation of equality and sharing hasn't worked for the same reason that Stalinism and Leninism haven't worked. You are a Socialist dictator trying to create equality and brotherly love by the power of the court, at the point of a switch. Our own U.S. Constitution states that *"all men are endowed by their Creator with certain unalienable Rights."* Webster's defines unalienable as *"not able to convey, sell, or make over (any property) to another."* It is a "self-evident truth:" each human being is endowed with rights that can not be surrendered to the jurisdiction of another. Your parental intrusion into these *unalienable* rights is as unwelcomed as the king's intrusion into the liberties of the colonies. Just as in a socialist state, your children will learn to use your intrusion as a tool to get their share of the pie. You have created a welfare state, taking from the haves to give to the have-nots.

Parent, how would you feel about your neighbors, or even your relatives, if the government forced you to give over rights to your bed or your lawn mower? Suppose that on your day off from work you came home to find your well maintained lawnmower already in use by your careless neighbor? You say to him, "Hey, I would like to use my lawn mower if you don't mind." He sticks his tongue out and jeers, "Nan Nan Nah Nann Nann, I got it firrrrrrst." So, do you say, "Well, I am supposed to give up my rights, and it is a law—share and share alike"? Is this how you build good relationships with your neighbors?

A parent must recognize the child's right to private property. The child must be allowed to possess his own property as he sees fit. If his right to be selfish is not recognized, then he does not have any rights. Again, a child can't give up rights he doesn't have. If there is a limit placed on his free use of those rights, then as long as he is operating under threat of loss of property, he actually never owns the property. He then must give over the property for fear of losing it. The property is not his, and when he gives it over he has given nothing, nor has he exercised benevolence. In selfishness he gives-over for the purpose of, in some measure, retaining usage of the thing that judicially is not his.

We should seek opportunity to teach the principles of giving and sharing, but our teaching should not be psychologically coercive. It is our desire to see our children have benevolent hearts. Forcing them to give will only rob them of the opportunity to freely give. They can only discover the blessedness of giving when it comes from their own hearts.

A child whines, “Make him play with me.” When you force unwelcomed associations upon your children, they do not learn to love each other. On the contrary, their despising only increases. How would you feel if you were forced to attend social engagements or spend the evening with someone not of your choosing? Would it endear that person to you if they had gone to the authorities whining of your indifference to them? When the authorities said, “Now you be sweet and let your neighbors sit in your house and gloat over their power to forcibly dominate your time, and remember you should give up your rights,” how would you feel toward you neighbor? And how would you feel about what you were doing? Would you have a good feeling that you had made sacrifices for your neighbor’s sake? No. You would be angry at everyone, and especially at the unjust authority.

There is an easy solution. Parent, put a stop to the bickering by allowing free associations. You can and should teach your children to be sensitive to the needs of others. But, as your children sense, you have no right to legislate or intimidate them into unwelcomed associations. To do so will prevent them from ever having a heart change toward others. If I see my neighbors, whom I may not particularly like, lonely or in need, I may choose to give up my rights and sacrifice my time to meet their needs. In so doing, I am drawn closer to them, not made resentful.

You may ask, “But what if when they are given their liberty, they chose to never associate with the other?” I do not think that is likely, for much of the bitterness and rejection is probably from the unjust intrusion of the one who is rejected. But if you are truly recognizing the child’s right to free association, then you must be prepared to allow the self imposed segregation. If it were possible for one child to dislike another so much as to never desire association, then it would be better for the rejected child to not have forced association with such a person.

Also remember that the whining child, who has learned to manipulate parents into forcing the other children to do his bidding, is of all children most despised and rejected by others. Furthermore, parents who reward whining soon cultivate such selfishness in their own children that they cannot help but despise "the brat." If you are angry and bitter toward your child, consider the probability that you are disappointed in your own creation.

The squabbling over property is even easier to deal with. Parents, you need to bring your children together and open a "land and title company." Cause your children to register each possession. Every toy, chair, bed, bedroom (or corner of a shared bedroom) should be designated as the sole property of one child only. If they have common property, divide the toys into two piles and let them draw straws for their pile. Oversee a period of trading (when they exchange toys on whatever bases they may agree upon) and then seal it with a "homestead act" that assures future "government" (parental) protection of those rights.

Small children should be trained not to touch the private property of older children. And older children should be given liberty to police their own property. When an older child is free to maintain control of his own property around his younger brothers and sisters, he is then free to relate to them as guardian and guide rather than competitor and victim.

No one has ever settled on my land or tried to manage my personal property, because there is no question but that the government guarantees my rights to private property. It doesn't matter who got there first or who was playing with my lawnmower first; if I can prove it is mine, there is no contest. There will be less resentment and feelings of unfairness. Your children will like each other better, if they are not forced into communal living.

If you will function as a government should (to protect rights, not redistribute them) then your children can relax their vigilance to grab and tightly possess. It will end the mad competition to get there first and hold on the tightest. It will be the end of argument. What is there to discuss? All property goes to the owner upon request, regardless of the circumstances. When Johnny whines, "He took my truck," instead of trying to reconstruct the squabble, you can simply say, "It is his truck. Give it to him."

Furthermore, where you have seldom seen your children give-up anything, under the private ownership policy, you will see individual acts of sharing begin to take place. When your children discover the good feeling of giving and the mutual benefit of sharing, they will begin to practice it at least as much as you do. By making this change in your tactics, by giving up the socialists power play, you will come to rely more on teaching and example. It should increase your awareness of your duty to exemplify in word and deed the Christian graces you seek to instill.

Not until their hearts are renewed by the Holy Spirit will they ever truly give out of pure love. If you allow them the free choice and God endowed liberties that are theirs, they will then, and only then, be free to develop morally in this area. Make a commitment to trust to your teaching and example, not to the legislation of "Big Brother." The curtain came down in Russia. It might as well come down in your home. ☺

The Bottom Line

I had left my wife at the airport, coming to this distant city to teach several seminars. My hosts showed me to an upstairs hallway where I was to sleep. It was a new and strange, but familiar place. My book would not be needed if all families were the quality of this one. I had been there one night, and arose before light to join the noisy activity. The five boys had more energy than a flock of black birds. I thought I knew all the ways a kid could mount a couch. Did you know you can sit on a couch with the back of your neck, your head pointing out, your face searching the ceiling for spiders, your rear where your shoulders are normally, and your feet in proper position, right side up but backwards? And all the time competing with a flock of brothers for space while the Bible story is being read? Don't ask for patience. God will give you five of those critters, all of the male variety, each thirteen months apart.

But in the midst of the circus, over by the heater, I saw a

five-year-old fellow lay his two-year-old brother on a blanket, hoist his legs, remove a very, all night long, three times over, soiled diaper and begin to wipe and wash away the night's litter. Very routinely and quite efficiently, the five-year-old held his little brother's two legs up with one hand and wiped with the other. He completed the task in record time and with optimum cleanliness.

I looked around in wonder to see which parent was going to start the brag, but no one had noticed. When I excitedly questioned, "How did you get him to do that?" the mother explained that one day he just decided it was his chore and assumed the responsibility. My wife worked on me for ten years and finally got me to change about three diapers of the number-two variety.

Can you conceive of the depth of caring and fellowship that existed between these two little brothers? Now you are waiting for me to give you the secret of training your five-year-old to change diapers. Well, I don't know yet. I am thinking about it. Maybe it's a quirk, but a pleasant one for this particular mother. ☺

Laying Down Habits

You might consider chickens to be on the lower end of the intelligence scale, though on the upper end of preference in the food chain. And you may be right; but as dumb as they are, they can still be trained. Like your children, chickens develop habits. Whether the habits are good or bad depends on their keeper. You are wasting your time to get mad at a flock of chickens. If you run at them shouting, they just squawk and scatter in as many directions as the number of drumsticks divided by two. They can't understand your words, so you are wasting your time fussing at them. When you bawl them out, they just look up from their constant pecking on the ground to see if you have any old corn bread. If not, they go back to eating dirt. After having chickens for quite a while, I will admit that they are not much more intelligent than a peanut butter sandwich, but they can be trained.

Chickens were created by God to provide farm fresh eggs. Regardless of what the experts say, it is their contribution to breakfast. Most of the time, chickens are kept in a small pen. You don't want them laying eggs all over the ground. Therefore, when you build a chicken pen you make several nests for their egg laying. The chickens like privacy when laying eggs, so early every morning they seek out these little elevated boxes with the soft straw. There, now you have trained the fowl creature to lay its eggs in a certain place. With forethought, you have caused a good habit to develop. But if you are careless you can untrain them.

Late in the day, farmers open the chicken coop door and allow the expectant egg layers, and one rooster, out into the yard. They learn to anticipate the time, and will stand in a group waiting to be released. The rooster runs out first to clear the ground of any intruders, but if it is a chicken hawk or stray poultry-plucking dog, he stops being a rooster and becomes just another chicken. Even stupidity has its limits.

Chickens generally lay their eggs early in the day, so you make sure that during that time they are in their pen close to their nest. If a chicken that has been released into the yard feels a need to lay an egg, it will return to the nest—as long as it is convenient. However if you consistently release the chickens before they have laid all their eggs, and they stray too far from the nest, they will develop the habit of laying their eggs on the ground. Once this practice becomes a habit, even when put back in their pen, they will stop climbing up to the nest and will continue laying their eggs on the ground.

My wife has a big heart when it comes to her chickens. All I have is a big stomach. The chickens learned to recognize her as the one who releases them. When she passes their pen early in the day, they take advantage of the opportunity to play upon her tender emotions. The rooster will lead the hens over to the door where they will stand bunched up like pitiful refugees waiting to be released. To satisfy her own need to show pity, Debi began a process of turning them out earlier and earlier. Then we started finding eggs in the yard. This forced my wife to ignore their pitiful manipulations and leave them in the pen where we would have all our eggs in one basket.

Well farmer, you have trained and then untrained your chickens. They started off with good habits and ended up with habits that destined them for a dumpling retirement. It won't do you any good to get mad at the dumb clucks for laying their eggs on the filthy floor. It will do no good to shame them and scream, "Don't you even care?" It will not help to force a comparison with the neighbor's well trained chickens. And it won't help to have more chickens if you haven't learned anything.

Now thankfully, your children are many times more intelligent than these chickens, and it is much easier to break them of bad habits. Although, they are much better psychologists than the pitiful chickens. Who is in charge of your children farm, you or the chicks? Your pity is not to the benefit of your children. It only feeds their desire to gain further control. Sit down and think about it; arrange circumstances to make the good habits convenient and the bad habits inconvenient. Persevere until the desirable action becomes ingrained, and then maintain order so that the good habit is always the convenient thing to do.

By the way, switches and rods make many things mighty inconvenient. ☺

The Folly of Fairness

By the time your children are ten to twelve years old, they should have developed the wisdom and skills necessary for good parenting. For several months now, our twelve-year-old daughter Shoshanna has been insisting that we address an issue that is disturbing to her. She finds this to be the most common problem of the small children she baby-sits. She sees the same traits in many of her own peers. She says, "Daddy, write and tell them that life is not fair."

There is a universal tendency to try to make life fair. "You had your turn, now it is mine." "You already have two balls and I have none, so you should be fair and share with me." "Daddy gave Johnny one, so Suzy should get one also." We tend to think of legislated fairness as equality, when in fact it is inequality. This is so ingrained in us that we equate fairness with justice. The communist system is built on a principle of forced fairness. In contrast, the American system of government is based, ideally, on justice.

Pure fairness is as unlikely and as undesirable as making all mountains the same height. It is unnatural and can only be achieved through forced injustice. When it is a rule handed down by "Big Brother" it will never be carried out with benevolence on the part of the one being stripped of his abundance, nor can it be received with thankfulness on the part of the one expecting legislated equality.

Jesus gave a parable that speaks about fairness and our attitude toward it:

> *"Matt. 19:1 For the kingdom of heaven is like unto a man that is an householder, which went out early in the morning to hire labourers into his vineyard.*
>
> *2 And when he had agreed with the labourers for a penny a day, he sent them into his vineyard.*
>
> *3 And he went out about the third hour, and saw*

others standing idle in the marketplace,

4 And said unto them; Go ye also into the vineyard, and whatsoever is right I will give you. And they went their way.

5 Again he went out about the sixth and ninth hour, and did likewise.

6 And about the eleventh hour he went out, and found others standing idle, and saith unto them, Why stand ye here all the day idle?

7 They say unto him, Because no man hath hired us. He saith unto them, Go ye also into the vineyard; and whatsoever is right, that shall ye receive.

8 So when even was come, the lord of the vineyard saith unto his steward, Call the labourers, and give them their hire, beginning from the last unto the first.

9 And when they came that were hired about the eleventh hour, they received every man a penny.

10 But when the first came, they supposed that they should have received more; and they likewise received every man a penny.

11 And when they had received it, they murmured against the goodman of the house,

12 Saying, These last have wrought but one hour, and thou hast made them equal unto us, which have borne the burden and heat of the day.

13 But he answered one of them, and said, Friend, I do thee no wrong: didst not thou agree with me for a penny?

14 Take that thine is, and go thy way: I will give unto this last, even as unto thee.

15 Is it not lawful for me to do what I will with mine own? Is thine eye evil, because I am good?"

The men that had worked all day for the agreed price of one penny recognized it was not fair to pay the same penny to those who had worked only one hour. They began the day expecting only one penny for the full day's labor. They had indeed been treated justly, but not fairly when compared to the others. Twice, the master of the vineyard said, "I will pay you what is right." The unfairness of pay is nonetheless called "right."

When our children complain of unfairness, it is because they feel they should have received more in respect to what someone else has received, exactly as these men in the parable. The response of the employer—typifying God—was to define their desire for equality as "evil." He vindicates his unequal actions by pointing out that it is lawful for one to do as he pleases with his own possessions. Their heart became evil when they coveted the increase of their neighbor.

When children complain of inequality they are being covetous, as seen by the fact that they never complain when they are on the receiving end, only when they are left out. If the parents give in to this complaining, they are rewarding their children's lust.

To cater to this equality syndrome is also to convey a very false concept about life. In the real world, what is mine is mine and what is yours is yours. If my neighbor has three cars when I have none, I can expect to walk. If he gives me a ride, I will be thankful, but I do not feel it is his duty to share. If he were forced to share, it would be impossible for me to have gratitude toward him.

Just this summer one of my younger daughters went canoeing with a visiting family of four teenagers. The youngest was a boy of thirteen. His mother, not having confidence that he could survive a spill in the swift water, told him to wear a lifejacket. His three, older teenage sisters were not so required. On the way to the canoe rental, as they stopped for gas, the boy went inside and called his mother, complaining of the unfairness of his sisters not having to wear life jackets. The mother relented to his pitiful appeal and told him that since he had to endure the discomfort of a lifejacket, they would have to also. After all, it was only fair. As they were preparing to leave the gas station, he came out gloating over his successful appeal to fairness. And parents wonder why their children don't like each other!

One of the girls got on the car phone and spoke to her mother about their distaste for wearing life jackets. The mother again relented and said that none of them had to wear a lifejacket. So the kid got his way after all. His mother obviously felt that he needed the jacket to insure safety, but she was forced to step back from her better judgment based on an assumption of fairness and equality.

If he had been my kid, every time he complained I would have put another lifejacket on him until he looked like a giant, orange flower floating down the river. He would have had so much buoyancy that if he had fallen in the river he would't have gotten wet. The next time I told him to wear a lifejacket he would have put it on so fast that those watching would have looked around for a tidal wave.

When the thirteen-year-old boy won the fairness contest over the lifejackets, do you think his sisters and the others present found him endearing? Do your children like each other, Mom?

This assumption that fairness is the "golden rule" seems to be universal. We see it on all sides. I noted an occasion when a mother was about to prevent her older teenage daughter from going with her peers because the younger sister was not also invited. The mother, finally allowing her older daughter to go, consoled the younger child by promising to take her someplace special to make up for the inequality.

Again, it is common to hear a small child complain to his mother, "They ran off and left me." The mother then scolds the older child, telling him to wait on his younger, slower brother. Does it cause the older boy to like the little brother who is allowed to cramp his more aggressive style of play?

This indulgent demand for fairness begins at the earliest age. You can know you have already cultivated self-centeredness in your children when Grandma must buy gifts of equal value for each grandchild in order to keep feelings from being hurt. Trying to keep equal accounts, whether in things, privileges, or discipline, is not wise. It trains children to believe they have the right to weigh and balance, to demand equal share, or to veto the good fortune of another. They are turning selfishness into a childhood occupation. Evil covetousness is being rewarded.

Parents are missing one of the greatest opportunities to teach their children to rejoice in the good fortune of another. The men of the parable who worked all day should have rejoiced that those who worked only one hour received as much as they. If they had been the one to work only one hour, they would have rejoiced. Their demand for fairness was pure covetousness. To give in to that demand is to cultivate your own "Entitlement Program."

It should never be our intentions to show favoritism, but circumstantial inequality is not only just but essential to the very foundations of individuality. Some are naturally tall, while others are short. Some are gifted in many areas, whereas others appear to be gifted in little. One farmer receives rain while another suffers drought. One is born into a family of opportunity while another is born into social bondage. One gets a promotion while another loses his job. Many run the race, but only one takes first place.

Premeditated inequality, which is what occurred in the parable, is often most appropriate. The Bible tells us to value the other person above ourselves. That's not equality. It's inequality in favor of your neighbor.

Remember, our goal for our children is not to make them happy by immediately gratifying their natural lusts; we want to build character. Children do not yet have a mature capacity to make wise value judgments. It would not be wise to provoke a child to wrath by deliberately showing preferential treatment. But it is equally unwise to seek equality by seeking to avoid inequality where it naturally occurs. For instance, if you are at a garage sale and come across a garment or toy suited to one of your children, it would be perfectly appropriate to buy for the one and not for the other. To deliberately seek equality is to send a wrong signal. The child who receives nothing should be able to rejoice in the good fortune of his brother. He would not feel that his mother loved the other more. He knows that the inequality is purely circumstantial. If one child is invited to participate in an event with his friends, and the other is not, it would be extremely unwise to attempt to make an offering to pacify the child left behind. It would be fine to take that opportunity for just the two of you to do something together, but not as a bribe for good attitude, nor as a consolation for his losses.

If a child is left out of play because the other children don't like him, it would be injurious to publicly take his side. He should learn to be likable. He must earn the right to be included in social events. Children will readily isolate a jerk. Protective parents, defending a child's rights, create super jerks. When he doesn't get his share of attention, time, things, or whatever, don't cater to his selfishness by becoming gravely sympathetic and sensitive to his feelings. Lighten up and show indifference to his feelings. Briefly and curtly, as you turn to walk away, say, "Stop your whining and find something to do, or I will give you a job to take your mind off of it." You might add, "When you get bigger, you will get to go places also."

One caution: We occasionally meet parents or stepparents who clearly do not like one child and so favor another. They express their preference in gifts and discipline. The children all know that one is despised and another is preferred. These parents may use what has been said to justify their ongoing vendetta against the rejected child. This kind of stupidity is not born of ignorance, but rather of meanness of spirit. Parents who are so blinded are not likely to discern the difference between just inequality and selfish preferential treatment. May these parents see the pain they are causing before their rejected child becomes a reject of society.

But if you are the average parent, you readily see the evil in deliberate preferential treatment. On the other hand, you may never have considered that your attempts at fairness were actually unjust and counterproductive in terms of character building. As a result of your renewed understanding, your future responses will be different.

When your child gets knocked down, don't reward his whining of unfairness. Teach him how to get up and walk away with dignity. If the other children run off and leave him, teach him how to organize play that will cause them to want to be a part of his activity. But never make your child the unwelcome tagalong of despising peers. When your child digs a well, and they take it away from him, teach him to dig a better well in another location, and God will bless him with better water. When rain falls on his neighbors' crops but not his, teach him how to irrigate. When his wages are lower, teach him how to manage his finances. When someone else gets the job, teach him how to start a company that provides better services. If he has fewer gifts, teach him how to expect nothing and to make little into abundance. Rather than whine for equality, teach him how to give until others are blessed above himself. If Christian principles are not good enough for our two-year-olds, will they be good enough for them when they are twenty? Cultivate a Christian worldview when they are young, and when they are old they will not depart from it. ☺

Tying Strings/Beards

Last week when I was mildly suffering from loss of a wisdom tooth, I drifted down to where some of the saints were playing volleyball. I plopped down into an old torn bucket seat someone had thrown out of his pickup truck. It is now front row seating, far more coveted than the stumps and lengths of firewood standing on end. As I sat there I tried to look pitiful, occasionally wincing from pain and thrusting my hand to my jaw. But I found the volley ball sideline to be a poor place to get sympathy.

Then two kids, children of those playing volleyball, spotted me seated alone. They made a dash to take advantage of me, certainly knowing my vulnerability. I had hoped that they would question me about my recent ordeal. I was all ready to tell them about the blood and suffering. But they were totally heartless. They continued to laugh and jump around like the world was a wonderful place. It would be several days before I would feel that way again.

They were expectant that I should jump up and provide them with the usual legs on which to climb. They think I am a tree house and my arms are swings. If these growing four- and six-year-olds keep swinging on my arms, I will probably have to buy shirts with longer sleeves. But I was not to be trifled with on this day. I just slumped deeper into the bucket seat and groaned my misery. They settled down, but instead of going away, they began to stroke my beard. Man, that's great solace for a toothache.

I became absorbed watching the ball game, when I suddenly realized that the kids were backing off and laughing at me. They would lean their heads to one side, much like an artist trying to study his creation. I noticed the little girl approaching with a stem of wild berries. She was coming toward my beard and her brother was saying, "Yea, that will look good!" I followed her until my eyes crossed about six inches from my nose. She commenced to braid the berries into my beard while the boy came back with a piece of Styrofoam to do the same. They were having so much fun, now squealing with delight, that I submitted to this lowly degradation until the grounds around the court were completely clean. When I got up to leave, I left a trail of raining debris that looked like the highway trail of a country garbage truck. And the kids were walking along behind me laughing at the stuff I was shedding.

Now you may have more dignity than I do, and you probably don't have a beard long enough to keep a couple of kids busy for twenty minutes. But I will tell you what I do have. I have two little friends. ☺☺

An Idea We Tabled

Up until recently, our family didn't sit down to the table, we sat down at a continent. My wife bought a perfectly clear tablecloth and under it she placed several large world and national maps. We grew fond of quizzing each other on obscure countries now owned by ex-CIA operatives. My boys came to know the rivers and mountain ranges of different countries. One day I came in to find the kids leaning over the map, all looking at the same spot, sounding as if they were competing for first place in a sports announcer's school. "There he goes across Turkey. He is now entering Iraq… No! He has turned North. He is entering Iran and making his way across to… No, he has jumped into the Persian Gulf and is entering Saudi Arabia…." They were following a bug across the world map. I thought it was a most effective homeschool method.

But last week we came to dinner to find the geographical maps replaced with thirteen full color posters of the human body. Now the Bible says that *"no man yet despises his own flesh but cherishes it and nourishes it."* I guess my wife thought there was no better place to observe the flesh than where we nourish it.

The boys quickly grew tired of observing the urinary tract during meal times. One afternoon, while eating a snack, I sat down where the boys usually sit and found I wasn't so hungry after two minutes of observing a bladder blockage. So I moved over one seat and tried to eat a bologna sandwich while looking at a dissection of the liver. The next meal, I moved around to the girls' side and studied stomach and colon cancers until I developed indigestion. I finally tried my wife's seat and studied the brain until I felt I needed a lobotomy. My position at the end of the table is graced by a ten inch eyeball, complete with all the vessels and muscles. It reminds me of a Vietnamese dish I once ate. Did you know that the Superior Rectus M. on the top and the Inferior Rectus muscle on the bottom enables your eye to look up and down? You didn't? How in the world can you read this newsletter then?

I have studied the eyeball until I feel the whole body is an eye. But I moved to the opposite end of the table and found the answer to that verse of Scripture which asks, "If the whole body were an eye where were the hearing?" Simple. It's at the other end of the table. We are trying to find where my wife hid the world maps. ☹

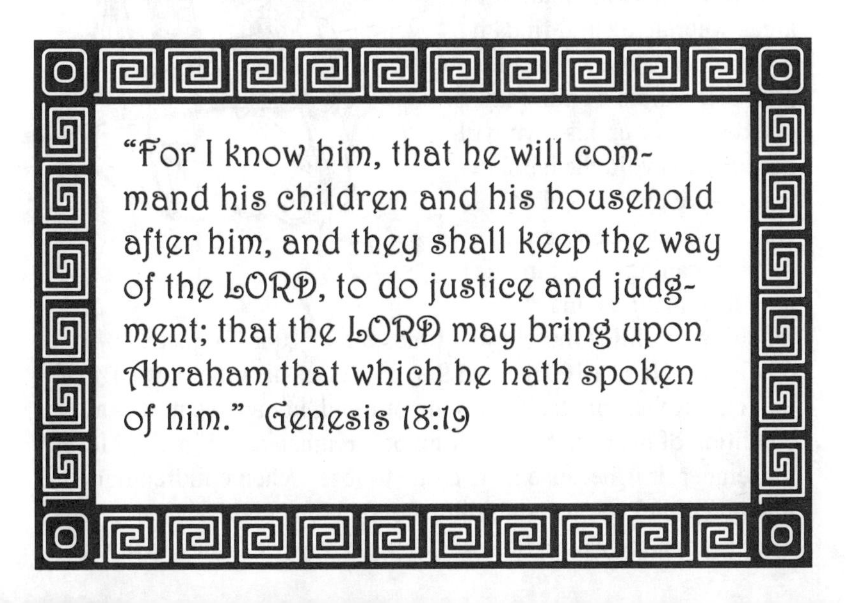

Sitting Down Inside

Several times I have been asked by parents how they can make a child sit in a car seat when he or she refuses to do so. Understand, our goal is not just to MAKE them sit in the car seat. Our goal is to TRAIN them to cheerfully comply. The parent is obviously big enough to force the child to sit in the car seat. But like one older kid said on a different occasion, "I may be sitting down outside, but I am still standing up inside." Our desire is not just to win the contest. We want to train them to sit down inside. As we look at this, we are not just discussing car seats, we are uncovering a principle that translates into all areas of child training.

When a child is rebellious only occasionally, even in a single area, you can be sure that you have a rebellious child. Don't be deceived by the fact that they are mostly obedient. There are many areas wherein a child finds it convenient to obey. Out of pure selfishness a child may decide to give up his own will, possibly to avoid the hassle that is sure to follow. But when an issue comes along that is meaningful to him, he may then manifest his rebellion. A child who obeys 9 times out of 10 is not just 10% rebellious. He is a 100% rebel that expresses his rebellion 10% of the time. Rebellion itself is a state of mind, not an event. It is a condition of heart, not a condition of circumstance. If a child loses his temper, it is because he had one to lose. When children burst into anger they are just dumping the load they regularly carry. We want to treat the cause, not the symptom. A switch may treat the

immediate symptom, but unless it is combined with effective training, it will not treat the source problem—the child's heart.

Our desire as parents is to build character into our children. The power play by itself is insufficient. We cannot forcibly invade the "command and control room" of their hearts. It is their sacred ground. No one, not even God, can get into the recesses of another person's soul unless invited in. A parent may be spanking or intimidating a child into outward compliance while, on the inside, the child's rebellion is actually growing.

A mother told her story: "Suzy has taken a notion that she doesn't want to ride in the car seat. Every time I tell her to get in, she refuses. I have spanked her, but she stubbornly stands there unyielding. I tell her that we are not going unless she gets in, and she still refuses. I called my husband out and he spanked her three times, but still she stubbornly refused to get in the seat. If we forcibly put her in the seat, she bucks and screams in defiance. I just don't know what else to do. I feel guilty about further spanking."

I asked this mother what she did after threatening to leave Suzy at home. She said she had no other choice; they went to the store with Suzy triumphantly standing as usual.

There are several preliminary things to consider:

First, ask yourself, "Is Suzy's cry one of dreadful fear or one of angry rebellion?" Any parent will immediately know the difference. It is a slim possibility, but one you must first consider: could it be that she has developed some negative associations with car seats? If so, the following solution would not apply. I will not take the space to discuss the solution to so rare a possibility, but it would be the easier problem to address.

Second, note that up until this point the mother above has actually trained Suzy to rebel. The hollow threat not to allow her to go has convinced Suzy that her mother is a liar. Just two or three more screams and Suzy always wins. She has been trained to hold out against threats. She has also been taught that if she can just endure two or three more spankings, she will eventually get her way. Her bottom is callused, but not as badly as her soul.

Third, note that her parents often depend on pain and threat alone to change Suzy's mind. She is supposed to be scared into compliance. However she has proven that she is tougher than either parent. Like a good rebel soldier, she can hold out against enemy torture and still maintain her pride. Her resolve is: "No one is going to break my spirit."

Fourth, note that in Suzy's mind the battleground has actually moved from the car seat to personal autonomy. Suzy is fighting a battle against the very concept of authority. She is learning early to resist all rule of law and to do only that which meets her fancy. This is a serious problem. The parents have already lost not only the battle, but the child. Because Suzy is yet young and the consequences of her rebellion can be contained or ignored, the immediate ramifications are minimal. But when she is fourteen, her parents will suddenly cry out, "Where did I go wrong?" They lost the whole battle when their little girl was only 18 months old. After that, they were just feeding and coddling an unthankful rebel until her day of throwing off the yoke.

Fifth, if the spanking is not working, especially if you feel guilty about it, don't stick with a solution that doesn't solve the problem. Spanking is only one part of a larger plan of child training. If all the other ingredients are missing, and you wait until everything is out of control and then jump in with the rod, you are asking the rod, which is only a part, to do the job of the whole. If you are trying to put a wheel on an axle, at some point it may be necessary to utilize the hammer, but if you rely on the hammer alone, without first lining up the wheel, you will not only fail to mount the wheel, you may damage it so that it can never be mounted. When a hammer is needed it is indispensable. When it is not needed, it is a clumsy hindrance. Unless your thinking is clouded by your own emotional imbalance, your own intuition will guide you as to the appropriateness of rod.

How might one effectively deal with this situation? Keep in mind that we want to knock at the door of the child's soul and cultivate in him or her a desire to please and to obey. If we don't get to the root, we have utterly failed. When we break rebellion in one area we have broken it all areas. The mind and heart must be persuaded, trained, conditioned, molded.

Certainly there is more than one way to effectively handle this scenario, but I will offer a solution that will provide us with insights into the principles we must come to understand. The key to developing a creative solution is to understand the motivation and methodology of the child. The parent wants the child to sit in the seat for the sake of safety. The child does not want to sit in the seat because it is not as much fun as standing. And then there is the element of autonomy. The rebel child intuitively recognizes the need to maintain an unbroken record of independence. To give in just once is to confirm the parent's decision to use the rod. It is to relinquish authority. Once the child has outwardly asserted her independence, she knows it is vital to all future confrontations to not yield her independence under threat. For the very same reasons, it is vital that you win.

But Suzy's mother has a secret weapon —the keys to the car. (Be grateful that Suzy is not yet able to drive.) Suzy's mother had the right idea when she threatened to leave her behind. But Mother was a cowardly liar. Here again is the principle: You train Suzy by denying her any gratification or success in her rebellion. **Make all rebellion counterproductive.** Determine what her goals are and arrange circumstances to thwart her efforts. Mother must appear the winner. She must be indomitable, unassailable, an unmoving rock of truth and righteousness. Mother's word must be written in stone, the *"law of the Medes and the Persians, which changeth not."*

So here is how you conquer. When Suzy refuses to get into the car seat, give her five licks with a stinging switch. Calmly command her to get in. If she doesn't, repeat the switching. After about three times, if you are confident that two are three more switchings are not going to cause her to yield, calmly tell her that hereafter she will never be allowed to ride in the car unless she sweetly gets into the restraining seat. Of course, she thinks you are the same old liar, so she will resolutely determine to outmaneuver you. Take her inside and call someone you trust to sit with her while you go to the store. Regardless of her screams and threats, cheerfully leave her behind. When you return, be sure to have chocolate on your mouth and a smile on your face. Sing as you bring the groceries in, and be sure to forget to purchase the things she always persuades you to buy. Explain to her that you were having so much fun, and without her along to remind you, you just failed to buy the things she likes.

Don't nag her about it. If you keep raising the issue, it may harden her resolve to hold out. Go on about your daily routine as normal. Do things with her that are fun, and let her know that you love her. The next day, get up excitedly talking about the trip the two of you are going to take today—someplace she likes to go. Walk to the car and prepare the car seat. Tell her to get in. If she refuses, spank her right there, and then take her back into the house. Call the babysitter and go have a great time. Come home in a party mood with a busted balloon hanging limply on the end of a stick. Tell her you sure did miss her at the mall, but maybe she will be able to go next time. Repeat this each day, one spanking and a short admonition before returning her to the babysitter, until she cheerfully gets into the seat with no complaint.

You have denied her success as a rebel. She has learned that to cross Mama is total futility. Mama is lord; she knows what she is doing. No one bests Mama—except Daddy.

When she climbs into the car seat of her own volition, without being driven into it with a switch, you have conquered her soul with light. Rebellion is crushed under the foot of Divine government—in the hands of Mama.

In the unlikely possibility that she continues to refuse, after, say, two weeks, take the car seat inside the house and tell her to get in. If she refuses, calmly use minimal force to strap her in. Designate a length of time that she must sit there, and then release her only when the time is up. Try to make it long enough for her to tire and cease rebelling (two or three hours). It is most effective if she is in a state of surrender when she is released. Repeat this until she grows out of the car seat, or until she willingly gets in. She will not continue her rebellion once she is convinced that it is futile.

One final warning: If you are torn up emotionally, harboring anger, pity, grief, sadness, or anything other than disinterested cheerfulness, the child may not surrender. By your upset spirit you are sending a signal that her terrorist tactics are effective. I once asked a man how he was able to train his dog so effectively. He replied, "Oh, you just have to be smarter than the dog." ☺

Carnal Husbands, Cranky Wives and Cantankerous Kids

by Debi Pearl

In our child training seminars there is always a time for questions and answers. It is during these times that we come to understand your needs. As parents begin sharing their different experiences, I am amazed at the similarities. The testimonies go something like this: "We are a family of more than average discipline. We home school, are active in church, and have family devotions. We have trained and disciplined the children from their youth, and I thought we were having good results until they got into their early teens."

Continuing, they tell us of the different ways their children have manifested their disrespect and dishonor. How can this happen? How can parents do everything right and still suffer rebellion in their teenagers? Does that verse mean, *Train up a child in the way he should go and when he is a teen he will be disrespectful, but when he is old he will come back and not depart again?*

Over the years, as I have listened to these mothers tell of their similar experiences, the source of their problem has become clear to me. If they could be objective for just a moment, they too would be able to see the solution. To get to the root, I ask these mothers, "Does your husband do anything on a regular basis that you feel might be detrimental to the family?" Invariably, they answer something like this: "YES, and I always knew it would weaken the family, and now this proves it." Then I ask, "How do you react? Do you meet eyes with the children and silently communicate your disappointment? Are they in any way aware of your martyrdom as you willingly "die to yourself" in resignation to your husband's clumsy spirituality? Do you in any way indicate that you are praying he will assume his role as spiritual leader?"

When I ask such questions, the atmosphere of the room

suddenly changes. The "strong spiritual women" look as if they lost their unction. How do they feel? Probably the same way they make their husbands feel—like a second class Christian.

Over the years, I have heard many women speak in front of their husbands about how they are praying God will have His way in their families. Or they will brag about what a wonderful sermon that was and how they want that in their home. As I stand there listening, I am embarrassingly aware that their husbands are being reduced to carnal nincompoops.

The man can't complain that his wife doesn't obey him, because she does. He can't say she speaks evil toward him, because she doesn't. He can't fault her in anyway. But he is often angry; he feels he is not respected and honored; he feels the fool. And somehow, for all her years of faithful prayer, he never becomes a mighty man of God. In front of the children, she patronizes him. She doesn't know it, and he can't explain it, but the kids grow up feeling it all the same. It reaps anger, frustration, belligerence, irritation in the dad, dislike among siblings, and in teens, disrespect for their mother. The Scripture tells us *"Every wise woman buildeth her house; but the foolish plucketh it down with her hands (Prov. 14:1)."*

The children are subtly being persuaded that the head of the house is not really the spiritual leader, and therefore not to be highly regarded—in fact he is a detriment to the growth of the family. No wonder when they become teens they treat their dad like the burden Mother has contrived him to be. Of course, when the children are young, Mom seems like a strong spiritual woman, but as they mature they look at her with the same critical eyes of judgment she has used on Dad. Every look of irreverence toward Dad is now multiplied and sent back her direction (Matt. 7:1-5). She has trained her children well in the folly of disrespect and irreverence. They might obey, because she has obeyed, but what is obedience without honor?

Mother, if you have a reputation as a fine Christian woman, yet lose your children to bitterness, what have you gained? Will it be satisfaction enough to be able to blame your husband?

The first and the most important thing you will ever do as a mother in training your children is to reverence your husband, delight yourself in him, love to obey him, feel honored to be married to him, joy in his presence. In doing so, you are building up your house, you are creating a home, you are establishing a foundation. This is the first and most important ingredient in raising happy, obedient, creative, respectful children, children who delight to be part of the family. This kind of atmosphere in the home causes your children to love each other, to enjoy being with their own brothers and sisters.

Oh, your teens might see that you are not Mr. and Mrs. Perfect, but they will delight in the fact that their parents really like each other. It makes for a very happy, peaceful home life. It makes the promises found in the Bible become a reality. It is the reason some parents who seem to do everything wrong are still able to raise good teens, while other parents who do everything right raise sour young people.

Ladies, we have in our grasp the opportunity to reverence our husbands, thus teaching our children how to reverence God. I can change eternity by choosing to delight myself in my husband, obeying him, loving him, and causing him to stand before God free from the shackles of domestic condemnation.

As Mike once said, "When a wife suggests that her husband take the lead, any leading he does after that is just following her suggestion." When you decide what course the family should take and then seek to bring your husband into conformity, you will not only spoil your marriage, but your children as well. If your husband is a 20% father and you make the children aware of your dissatisfaction, you will have 20% kids; but if you respect and honor your 20% husband, causing the kids to think you see him as 100%, you may have 100% kids. And a husband and father who is treated with honor and respect will rise to the calling and be more of the man he needs to be. ☺

Sunday School at Cane Creek

Five- to seven-year-old boys are like the rain; they are seldom convenient. In our church here at Cane Creek there are several boys in this age group. I have watched them grow from precious infants to cute babies to tumbling toddlers to talkative tykes. But by the time they are five, six, or seven they are… shall we say… unpredictable. You learn to view life from their three-foot perspective or you grow into a grouch.

Just as you began to get adjusted to the strange personality of the other adult with whom you share your life, along came this exploding new soul. He was so cute and dependent, and now he is a…boy. We begin our church assemblies with everyone attending the children's meeting. The children sit together at the front and participate, while the adults observe. This past Sunday was typical. Prior to the meeting, two of the boys, six and seven years old, had gathered several fuzzy, horned worms. They were the envy of the other children as they went around allowing privileged peeks into their cupped hands. By the time the meeting started, I had lost track of their worm zoo. Then one of the little fellows was called forward to lead one of the songs. He was trying to lead "Jesus loves the little children" in a Chinese dialect, followed by the same song in Spanish. It was a job difficult enough without trying to wrangle a herd of wild worms. But when the song leader saw that he was having trouble, she must have thought it was his squirming hands that were the problem, so she knocked them down at his side.

Sitting closer than anyone else, I could see what the others could not. I watched this creepy creature slowly crawl up his arm. He was trying hard to stand still and maintain his composure. I don't know what was happening on his other side, but when one worm disappeared under his short sleeve, I was squirming myself. We both began to shiver about the same time. His eyes were rolling around like spilled apples in the back of a pickup truck. However, he finished his songs in good form, and then bravely walked to his seat, where he commenced to dig through his clothes. I don't know if he ever recovered all the maverick worms, but seeing him endure that wild ordeal so calmly, I am convinced that we have the best six-year-old primitive missionary training program in the world.☺

Channel 23

A modern Psalm taken from "The New International Unchristian Perversion."

The TV is my shepherd, I shall not want anything else. It maketh me to lie down on the sofa. It leadeth me away from the Scripture. It destroys my soul. It leadeth me in the paths of sex and violence for the sponsors sake. Yea, though I walk through the valley of the shadow of death, I will enjoy the evil, for blood and sex they excite me. It's cable and remote, they comfort me. It prepares a commercial before me in the presence of my children. It anoints my head with humanism. My coveting runneth over. Surely laziness and ignorance shall follow my family all the days of our lives, and we shall dwell in the house watching TV forever.

But don't worry parents, as you know, the T.V. doesn't have any influence on the children of parents who don't want it to influence them. That's why the sponsors only advertise products you have already decided to buy. ☺

More Sibling Squabbles

Children attempt to control their environments, which means the people around them, through pity or threat. Most children come to rely on one approach more than the other. One child will display anger and threat, while another just looks broken and hurt. Though the angry child appears to be the most aggressive and intolerable, the two approaches are equally selfish and equally repugnant. The one will grow up trying to settle all personal conflicts in an explosive manner; the other will grow up to whimper and have "tender feelings." Of course, some of us have grown up to become versatile, employing combinations of anger and emotional manipulation. Regardless of whether the lever is anger or pity, the end is the same: to get one's own way, to be gratified in the senses, to take what the other has. It is the lazy, selfish, self-centered approach to life.

The self-centered child is marked by constant conflict. I repeat: the self-centered child or adult is marked by constant conflict—self-centered children, self-centered teenagers, self-centered mothers and fathers, self-centered preachers and churches, etc. Conflict is a clashing of interests, a difference of opinion as to who should be placed first, who should be most highly regarded. Children all want to be first. They want the most, the best; they want it now. At what age do they grow out of this? Somewhere around seventy or eighty, when their flesh dies. Nothing can stop it other than the sanctifying work of Christ, though early training can awaken the conscience to such a high state and discipline the soul to such a degree as to cause the child to grow into adulthood functioning in a most gracious and saintly manner. If you are the primary caretaker of a young child, you have the power, with the grace of God, to mold an eternal soul into the beauty of holiness.

What do you do with kids who just can't get along, who fuss and fight all the time? The atmosphere is punctuated with, "Stop!" "No!" "Give it to me." "Maaamaaa." To exacerbate the problem, most parents take the side of the younger child, or the girl, who is usually perceived as the weaker one. Parents feel compelled to rush to the defense of the one who appears helpless, the one whose selfishness is manifested in hurt feelings and a persecution complex. The other child appears aggressive, but in reality they are both aggressively using their best weapons to get their own ways.

It is a mistake to interpret conflict in terms of aggressor and victim. Occasionally that is the case, but not usually. Children are as smart as they are selfish. The ones who don't have the personality or brawn to rule through intimidation will soon discover the power of playing the victim, thus eliciting parental power to gain an advantage over their more explosive brothers and sisters. If the parents are blind to this ploy and are always intervening on behalf of the "victim," they will increase the tension, making a solution impossible. The one playing the victim and manipulating parents into running defense will just become more selfish; and the aggressor will

become more and more angry as he or she feels the injustice. I see some families where the parents treat all their children as victims of the outside world. Everyone is an aggressor, treating their children unfairly. The parents constantly run interference to see that their children are not mistreated. Talk about conflict! Families with this persecution complex are constantly on edge.

When sibling conflicts are settled by parents becoming arbitrators, ruling in favor of one child and against the other, kids learn to use it as opportunity to gain ascendance over their fellows. It is a game where the children are contestants. The parents are the "wheel of fortune." The children only need begin a conflict, and there is the possibility of coming out on top. "You win some, you lose some." Sometimes the game is played for recognition. "See me, I am the persecuted one! Give me your attention. Love me more."

Some children learn to manipulate their parents better than others. Deb and I were visiting in a home where this was so vividly played out. I try to appear to be listening to the adults, but I am usually observing the children. During breakfast, I saw the constant strain between the two children, a three-year-old girl and a four-year-old boy. The little girl, having awakened bright and cheerful, was sitting at the table full of playful mischief. The mother awakened the little boy and carried him to the kitchen table, still sluggish with sleep and cuddled in his mother's lap. Seeing the entrance of her brother, the little girl's contentment disappeared and was replaced by a sleepy whimper, as if she were full of scary emotions. Mama sat little brother down and picked up sister. As soon as sister was snuggled into Mama's lap, she threw her brother a smirking "ha ha" look. When the mother left the table, the little girl continued to do small, almost unnoticed offenses that irritated the older boy.

Later, while the mother was talking, I could look past her and see the two children playing. The cute little girl was obviously smarter than the clumsy brute of a boy. She was poised and controlled, while he was explosive and violent. Behind their mother, the boy was trying to put the top on a castle he had constructed. The little girl "assisted" and mischievously caused the castle to tumble. The boy, having had his fill of this little irritant, went into a rage and struck his sister. I could see it was only a token blow, but she began to cry as if she had suffered first degree assault and battery. The mother, responding to the crying, turned around to see the poor little girl sitting on the floor in the midst of a broken castle, the victim of abuse. Standing over her was her angry assailant quaking with rage. He couldn't explain his helpless feelings of injustice. But he knew that she had won again. He was carried into his room and spanked for bullying his poor little sister. As soon as Mother was out of sight, the little girl stopped crying, looking as if she had never cried at all, and smiling, said, "Brother is getting a spanking."

We frequently see this sort of conflict in families. If this mother came to us for counsel, the boy would be the focus of her concern. She would tell how she had spanked him and made him say he was sorry, but he only grew worse. The boy's rage was a result of his feelings of misuse. Certainly he had the normal amount of selfishness, but nowhere near as much as the "tender" little girl. Taking pleasure in his spankings, she was actually more violent than he. Lacking brawn, with calculating coldness, she just used her mother as the hit man.

What can a parent do to break into this cycle and put a stop to it? As we have pointed out, the parents' response is usually a part of the problem. Parents are thinking, "I just need to intervene more, spank more," when in reality, the children would be better off if the parents did nothing. As we have said, by arbitrating in favor of one or the other, parents are offering children the chance to gain ascendancy over one another. The parent who tries to discern which kid is at fault, punishing one and rewarding the other, is providing a continuing opportunity for sibling squabbles. The children are masters at bringing a situation to a head with just the right scream or cry, which is a signal for the arbitrator to make an entrance.

So, if I as a parent am making the situation worse with my arbitration, should I do nothing? Doing nothing is not the only alternative to constant arbitration. There will be times when you must hear both sides and make a judgment, but it should be only occasional. Just make sure that when you do arbitrate, both sides feel they would have been better off if they had settled it themselves. Remember, the rule in child training is: **Always make their negative behavior counterproductive.** Determine what, in their passion or lust, they hope to gain from this, and see to it that the opposite occurs. When two children fight over who got the chair first, leave the chair idle for the evening. When they fight over who is responsible for the mess in the bedroom, let one clean it up and then mess it up again and let the other one clean it up as well. If they are always fighting over the swing set and the slide, put tape on it, which declares it off limits for one day or one week until they both can come to you and declare that they have worked out a system to share.

When two of our children developed bad attitudes and started coming to Deb every half hour to tattle on the other, Deb just spanked both of them regardless of who did the tattling. No one ever said I sired dumb kids; they quickly discerned that the best course of action was to mind their own business. If your children learn not to bring their complaints to you, but continue to argue, listen until you discern what each hopes to gain and then deny each of them their desired indulgence.

One mother told how she dealt with two boys who just seemed to have constant personality clashes. It appeared they just couldn't stand each other. Now, according to our rule of child training (determining what, in their passion or lust, they hope to gain from this, and see to it that the opposite occurs), how would you cause these two boys to experience more of what they despised, which was each other, and less of what they wanted, which was distance? She taped their arms together, the left arm of one to the right arm of the other, shoulder to shoulder—and that with a sense of humor, not anger. Imagine these two enemies trying to coordinate every action to just perform the daily functions. She has some funny stories to tell. The boys think it's funny now. I won't tell you what happened when they tried to go to the bathroom. Can you see them trying to cooperate in buttoning and zipping, or pulling up an extra chair so the other can sit down? They had to cooperate to even walk through a door. Imagine them trying to dress, tie shoes. They soon began to see the humor in it and sought to cooperate just for the sake of survival. Today, the boys, now several years older, can laugh and tell of their experiences together without fighting over who was the best one-handed zipperer.

A father told how he dealt with two sibling enemies. When they just couldn't tolerate each other any longer, he made them stand facing each other with their noses touching. It makes my eyes cross just to think about it.

"Oh, your breath stinks."

"Yours smells like that dead cat we found in the tool shed."

"Don't press so hard; you're making my nose flat."

"Boy, my eyes are crossing."

"When I look to the side, one eye is still seeing you."

"Ugh, I'm getting dizzy."

"I wish you were as tall as me, my back is starting to hurt."

"Well I have to stand on my tip toes to keep your nose off my forehead."

"Don't talk so much; you just slobbered on my chin."

"It's a good thing neither of us has a cold."

"I told you we should have settled it before Daddy heard us."

"Yea, listen to him and the girls laughing."

"What are you laughing at now?"

"I was just thinking how funny this will look if we are still standing here when the postman comes. They will probably haul us off to one of those foster homes."

"Oh, Mama will let us stop before he comes… She will, won't she?"

We are not suggesting that you implement either of these methods; we just want you to see the principle involved. Again, the principle in training is to make the negative behavior counterproductive. Children who are so tired of looking at each other that they want to fuss and fight will think twice before risking a nose to nose confrontation. Children who have made it a way of life to complain of abuse will find it inadvisable to protest anything less than bloodletting when they know complaining brings deprivation and disapproval rather than sympathy.

You must relax so that your creativity can come forth. Never lose your sense of humor. Never allow yourself to cease to delight in your children. When their behavior is undesirable, ask yourself, "What do they hope to gain? What is their selfish motivation?" And then come up with a creative solution that will cause them to choose a different course of action the next time. If crime didn't pay, there wouldn't be any criminals. If children don't profit from fighting and quarreling, they will choose another course.

One caution: This "cause and effect" principle assumes that you have provided a nourishing environment, a home of love and honesty. If parents are always fighting with each other, they will fight with the kids as well. If you have lost dignity with your marriage partner, you will not relate to your children in dignity. Remember, more is caught than taught. ☺

Dear Pearls

In my attempts to be what one author terms a "Gentle Parent", my little girl could bring me to my knees in frustration and anger. When I finally did resort to a spanking, I felt like I was reflecting my parent who was out of control and had beaten me. The information in your book, when applied here in our home has not only removed from me the fear of being a reflection of my parent, but has allowed a feeling of loving control and training to come to our home. I was the emotionally weak mother who was afraid to turn my child's favor against me, for fear of losing her affection. Instead, as your book states, she has fallen more in love with me. The wooden "Spankyspoon" that we use is almost like her friend. Our marriage has been greatly strengthened through our uniting in our child-raising theories."

From Kentucky

And, ye fathers, provoke not your children to wrath: but bring them up in the nurture and admonition of the Lord. Ephesians 6:4

Bound

by Debi Pearl

I often ask myself, "Have they chosen to be bound?" Though I know in my heart that no one, not even the insane, chooses to be bound. Then why do they remain so? As I look out over the crowd of fettered couples, I wonder, do they even know of their bondage? I see pampered flesh, pious faces, composed emotions, and disciplined wills concealing the self-imposed bondage. Yet, on occasion, the pretense fails and their souls are seen through the bars of their making.

I look to my husband seeking the answers in his face, while silently whispering a prayer for him to have the wisdom he needs for so great a task. Can he say something that will cause them to see that the web binding their families is of their own spinning? Will he be able to tell this critical wife, wrapped in thick cords of bitterness, silly imaginations, contempt for her man, and romantic emotions, which she thinks is spirituality, that the cords binding her husband, chords she so despises, are cords she tied?

Like Eve, she plucks the fruit of bitterness, shares it with her husband, and then decries his lack of leadership. His lack of confidence before God and man, the apparent lack of interest in studying the Word, and his hesitancy to lead the family are not cords of his own making; they are cords she tied through her dissatisfaction with him as a man. He doesn't understand what binds him. His anger at circumstances he doesn't understand and can't seem to master drains his confidence before God. How can he soar before a mighty God if he can't please his own wife? They are *"heirs together of the grace of life,"* but they can never maintain a togetherness long enough to inherit. So their children must face life without the grace of life. What hope have they?

The woman sees couples where the man is mighty, he is confident, he receives honor from many. She feels his magnetism and manhood as he looks at his wife and smiles. "How can it be that that woman should get a mighty man of God, such a loving husband?" She can't understand why life should have permitted her such fate. She has so much talent, so much poise. She is ready to minister, but she must drag her husband along.

The wife goes to women's meetings and "shares" the sad story of her enslavement to a "carnal, insensitive husband." She bemoans the mistakes she made when she was less "spiritual." Now she suffers the consequences of having "married the wrong man." But she bravely "dies to herself" and lets her husband know of her longsuffering – with an emphasis on the suffering. She makes sure he is aware of the time she puts into prayer and Bible study.

She grieves over her lost opportunity and dreams of what it would have been like if she had only married a strong, mighty man, a man known for his wisdom. Does she not know her man could be all of that if she only allowed him to be free? Like Delilah cutting away Samson's strength, she cuts her husband and leaves him exposed to the Philistines of this world. Any man she married would soon pale in her eyes, because he, too, would be weakened by her criticism. After she cuts down her husband, her dissatisfaction grows, and she seeks out others to condemn or control. Other men, her children, and eventually the church leaders feel the sting of her tongue.

As I look across the room, how many in the audience are so entangled? It is sad, the mockery of this enslavement. More than anything, the wife wants her husband to be a "spiritual man"; and more than anything, he wants to please and serve the living God. Why then doesn't someone, anyone, just tell them about the cords that bind their spirits, slowly squeezing abundant life from their relationship? Why doesn't someone loose them? Perhaps someone has tried, tried many times.

Dear Sister, are you one of those in my audience who have allowed your bindings to enshroud your husband? Have you stolen his manhood with your discontentment? Would you release him?

As a man whose hands are tied, it might take awhile to get circulation flowing again, but it will flow. Will you tell your heart and soul to leap with joy and delight when you think of your husband? Will you enjoy the thrill of not only serving him but blessing him with absolute abandonment?

No wonder you don't feel loved. He is not free to love. His job is not to serve you; and your job is not to see to it that he does. Dear Sister, put away the things that bind you, and God will show you what a wonderful, delightful, precious relationship you can have on this old planet Earth. The things you are missing are beyond explanation. When I looked out over the audience, I whispered, "God, how do I tell them there is light when all they have ever known is darkness? How can I tell them to cut the cords when they think it is someone else who is bound?" ☺

The Power of the Media

If you come to the Church which is at Cane Creek and maybe hang around the volleyball court with your children, then you are eventually going to become the "star," disreputable or otherwise, of one of our newsletter articles.

This week in our community, a little seven-year-old boy came to his mother and with cautious concern asked, "Mama, am I going to be in Mike Pearl's newsletter?" This family is not part of the local church, and I haven't seen that little fellow in years, so the question must have been strange to his mother. She asked, "Why do you think you are going to be in the newsletter?"

With foreboding, he then related an event that occurred earlier when he was playing with Clint, his seven-year-old cousin, whom I see nearly every day. As the story was told by Clint's mother, here is what happened. Clint and his cousin developed a conflict of interests with ensuing verbal differences resulting in heated debate over personal priorities—nothing novel for two seven-year-olds. Their discussion was the foundation on which philosophy, dogmatic religion, and civil law are eventually forged. So Clint, with the brilliance of a logical tactician, resorting to his best argument, said, "If you don't..........then I am going to tell Mike

Pearl and he will put you in the newsletter." That did it. Clint's threat won the day. What a deterrent! But I am afraid we are developing a new kind of childhood phobia. It will probably end up in the first year psychology books as "Publication exposure schizoid hyper self-imposed discipline mania."

Several months ago we discovered another, far quicker, deterrent to public displays of negative emotion, otherwise known as throwing fits. We were keeping a little four-year-old girl when, to get her way, she suddenly resorted to her old standby tactic. She stiffened and commenced to scream hysterically. It was obviously designed to cause us distress and deep concern—a poor judgment on her part. She looked as if she were totally lost to the insensitive world around her, submerged in her own vortex of emotional suffering and anguish; but not so much that she didn't hear Deb say to Gabriel, "Go get the video camera, we need a picture of this." She turned it off faster than a popped balloon, sat up, and asked, "Why are you getting the camera?" Deb answered, "Oh, we are making a video on child training and we just need a few shots of kids throwing temper tantrums." And then, with the arrival of the camera, Deb gave her the nod to resume her display, saying, "Go ahead." As they all stood waiting, camera poised, faces anticipating good footage, the little girl, in a most controlled voice said, "No way," and walked off with the utmost display of dignity and self-control. The best we can discern she just didn't want the publicity.

Do you suppose these out-of-control kids could really gain control of their emotions if they had sufficient motivation? The psychologist may dub this one "Panasonic Panoramic Paranoia." Who knows, a ready camera could rid us of Ritalin—or perhaps just a threat to make their pictures and stories available to this newsletter would do the job. Send me your story. I will keep the names anonymous if you don't think you can stand the publicity. ☺

Child Training Precept

Never reward the child's lusts.

Never allow negative behavior to be rewarding.

Unbound

Dear Mrs. Pearl,

I literally just finished reading your article entitled, "Bound" in the February '97 newsletter, and I felt compelled to write to you before I even set the newsletter down. I am writing not only to thank you, but to commit myself to the accountability that comes from acknowledging my own sin and attitude to another person. That article was about me. My husband is a man of God, desperately struggling to please me, and feeling frustrated by his ineffectual life. As I read your article, I realized that I created his bondage in my attempt to motivate him to do things my way—to meet my selfish imaginations and romantic expectations.

Everything in me wants to go into the detail of the downward spiral our family has experienced in relationships—husband/wife; parent/child; family/church, etc. All the time, with me convinced that my husband isn't taking responsibility and seeking and following God. What incredible conviction!

I purpose, this very minute, to allow God to make me painfully aware of the looks, attitudes, words, and actions that either tear down or bind up my husband. I covet your prayers and pray for your continued willingness to be used by God to make these spiritual truths so obvious. Thank you. No one has ever dared to tell me so personally what I have done to create the situation I so vocally bemoan.

Tonight, I will greet my husband with joy and delight, and I will decide to think of him fondly and with respect. I will control my attitude and my actions. I will pray for and extol my husband publicly and privately. I will set an example of honor for our sons. I will repent of my sin toward my husband.

I will write again in the coming months and share the transformation I am sure our family will experience, with God's grace.

From Texas

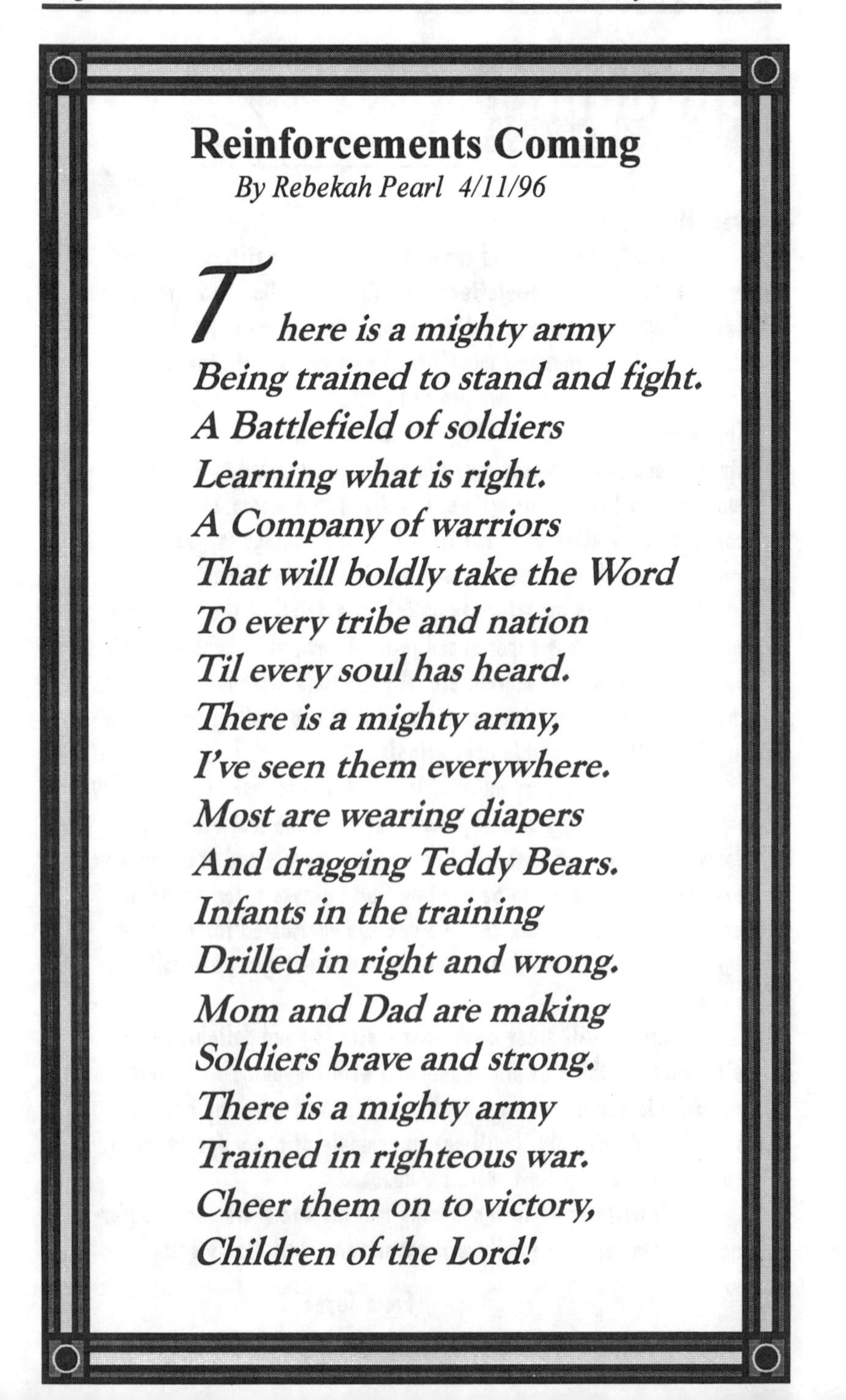

Reinforcements Coming

By Rebekah Pearl 4/11/96

There is a mighty army
Being trained to stand and fight.
A Battlefield of soldiers
Learning what is right.
A Company of warriors
That will boldly take the Word
To every tribe and nation
Til every soul has heard.
There is a mighty army,
I've seen them everywhere.
Most are wearing diapers
And dragging Teddy Bears.
Infants in the training
Drilled in right and wrong.
Mom and Dad are making
Soldiers brave and strong.
There is a mighty army
Trained in righteous war.
Cheer them on to victory,
Children of the Lord!

Index

Order Form

	Quan.	Code	Description	Suggested gift EACH	Total
BOOKS		BK 9S	To Train Up A Child 1-7 books	4.00	
		BK 9X	To Train Up A Child 8-99 books	2.50	
		BK 9C	To Train Up A Child Box of 100	2.20	
		BK 1S	No Greater Joy Volume One 1-7 books	4.00	
		BK 1X	No Greater Joy Volume One 8-99 books	2.50	
		BK 1C	No Greater Joy Volume One Box of 100	2.20	
		BK 4	Me? Obey Him? pbk. 95 pg. (Christian wives)	2.00	
		BK R1	Rebekah's Diary, pbk. 108 pg.	4.00	
			Ask for our free monthly newsletter		
AUDIO TAPES & CDs		AD 9	To Train up a Child (3 tapes read by Michael Pearl)	9.00	
		AD 1	No Greater Joy Vol. 1 (3 tapes read by Michael Pearl)	9.00	
		AD 10	Vinyl album of both books, To Train up a Child & No Greater Joy V. 1 (six tapes)	18.00	
		AD 11	Best Homeschooling Ideas (by Debi Pearl)	3.00	
		AD 12	Gami Akiz *told by Rebekah Pearl*	3.00	
		AD 13	Five Helpers *for women only*	3.00	
		AD 14	Authority and Prayer *sermon by Michael Pearl*	3.00	
		RB 02	From the End of the Earth *Cassette Music*	5.00	
		CD 01	From the End of the Earth *CD Mucis*	8.00	

The Church at Cane Creek
1000 Pearl Road
Pleasantville, TN 37033

Sub Total	
Postage	
Total	

SHIPPING

$0.01 - $10.00 ...... add $2.00 S/H
$10.01 - $25.00 .... add $3.00 S/H
$25.01 - $50.00 .... add $4.50 S/H
$50.01 - $100.00 .. add $6.00 S/H
$100.01 or more ... add 6%

- *No phone in orders.*
- *No COD's*
- *No charge cards*

All foreign orders triple **S/H**

Please print your name and address clearly.